CHAPTER ONE
EDITOR'S
PICKS

Ambleside

EDITOR'S PICKS | FOR MORE INFO, SEE P15 |

Ambleside has a rich Roman history, with a fort named Galava, dating from AD79 and situated just south of the town. Today it serves as a base for those exploring the surrounding countryside and is particularly popular with climbers, hikers and mountain bikers.

1

Haverthwaite Station

EDITOR'S PICKS | FOR MORE INFO, SEE P11 |

Visit a bygone age by climbing aboard a steam train at Haverthwaite Station and enjoy the stunning views across Lake Windermere. The Furness Railway was developed during the 1850's and 1860's, at the height of the Industrial Revolution, to transport coal and iron ore from the coastal mines to the heavy industries of the North West and North East of England.

2

Chesters by the River

EDITOR'S PICKS | FOR MORE INFO, SEE P63 |

Chesters by the River is situated in an enviable position with a deck overlooking the River Brathay. With a counter brimming with some of the finest looking cakes and brownies we ever did see, this contemporary restaurant offers rainbow salads and pizzas and flatbreads from its wood fired oven.

3

Crummock Water

EDITOR'S PICKS | FOR MORE INFO, SEE P24 |

Walking from the car park, the woodland dramatically opens up with incredible views of Crummock Water and over Grassmoor, Rannerdale Knotts, Mellbreak and Red Pike. Wild water swimming is popular in this lake and the more adventurous can take the (at times challenging) nine mile walk around the lake.

4

Lakeland Motor Museum

EDITOR'S PICKS | FOR MORE INFO, SEE P157

Lakeland Motor Museum has over 30,000 exhibits from around the world and chronicles the history of motoring through the twentieth century. The museum is a fantastic homage to the internal combustion engine and is housed in a converted mill. On display are cars, motorbikes, pedal cars, bicycles and the occasional unique machine.

5

Cartmel Cheeses and Bakery

EDITOR'S PICKS | FOR MORE INFO, SEE P133

Cartmel Cheeses & Bakery is one of the delightful businesses nestled within Unsworth Yard. Unsurprisingly given its name, the shop specialises in a wide range of British, Irish and French cheeses and freshly baked goods. It makes an ideal stop to gather a few picnic nibbles for a day out exploring the Lake District.

6

The Punch Bowl

EDITOR'S PICKS | FOR MORE INFO, SEE P53 |

The Punch Bowl is situated in the heart of the unspoilt Lyth Valley at Crosthwaite in Cumbria. Offering a 'unique blend of old and new,' The Punch Bowl is a luxurious country restaurant offering quality dining and stylish accommodation. Flickering fires, oak beams and polished oak floors only enhance the ambience.

7

Lingholm Kitchen

EDITOR'S PICKS | FOR MORE INFO, SEE P62 |

The Octagonal walled garden sits on the same spot as the old Lingholm Kitchen gardens which Beatrix Potter credited as her inspiration for Mr McGregor's garden in The Tale of Peter Rabbit. Built in a Victorian style, the garden has herbaceous borders while central areas are reserved for vegetable production which are then served fresh in the Kitchen.

8

Merienda

EDITOR'S PICKS | FOR MORE INFO, SEE P81 |

Merienda is an exceptionally stylish and contemporary licensed restaurant/café serving breakfast and brunch through to an eclectic evening menu. With a simple, globally influenced menu, the founders' aim has been to use wholesome, seasonal ingredients whilst drawing inspiration from around the world.

9

Coniston

EDITOR'S PICKS | FOR MORE INFO, SEE P10 |

Coniston was historically famous for its ore and slate mining. During Victorian times, the Furness Railway terminated in Coniston which opened up tourism to this beautiful area. Today hill-walking, rock-climbing and boating are popular pursuits from the village base.

10

Three Hares

EDITOR'S PICKS | FOR MORE INFO, SEE P94 |

The Three Hares is a family run seasonal and locally sourced café, bistro and bakery situated in the book town of Sedbergh at the foot of the Howgills. The cooking style here is influenced by the founders' appreciation for local wild food and their youth in Germany growing up with Japanese parents.

11

Gillams Ulverston

EDITOR'S PICKS | FOR MORE INFO, SEE P65 |

Gillam's Tea Room and Specialist grocer is an institution in Ulverston, with The Gillam family having provided fine food and excellent service in Ulverston since 1892, when John James Gillam opened his cash and wholesale grocers on Market Street. Today the tearoom offers wholesome home-cooked food made from local produce and the grocery sells organic fruit and vegetables, with an emphasis on provenance.

12

The Moon & Sixpence

EDITOR'S PICKS | **FOR MORE INFO, SEE P79** |

The Moon and Sixpence is an artisanal coffee shop in Cockermouth which has built a strong reputation for its high quality coffee and home-baked pastries. The owner, Stephen Kidd has immersed himself in coffee culture and even lived in one of the world's coffee capitals, Vancouver where he gleaned experience from the experts.

13

The Lakes Distillery

EDITOR'S PICKS | **FOR MORE INFO, SEE P31** |

The vision of The Lakes Distillery is to create one of the leading malt spirits in the world, alongside one of the most unique visitor experiences in the Lake District. Located in a converted Victorian cattle farm, the creation of this world-class production facility of quality spirits was a labour of love.

14

Honister Slate Mine

EDITOR'S PICKS | **FOR MORE INFO, SEE P113**

Honister Pass runs between Buttermere and the Borrowdale valley with fantastic views. At the summit is the famous Honister Slate Mine, which has been running for over 300 years. At Honister there are multiple unique activities to get your blood racing. These include Via Ferrata (extreme cable climbing) mine tours and the infinity bridge.

15

Grasmere Gingerbread Shop

EDITOR'S PICKS | **FOR MORE INFO, SEE P138**

The Grasmere Gingerbread Shop was established by Victorian cook Sarah Nelson in 1854. The reputation of her delicious gingerbread quickly gained traction and today the shop's famous clientele includes Hollywood actor Tom Cruise. This tiny shop was Sarah Nelson's Church Cottage home and remains almost untouched to this day.

16

The Bakery at No.4

EDITOR'S PICKS | FOR MORE INFO, SEE P70 |

Based in Kendal, The Bakery at No.4 specialises in making beautiful bespoke wedding cakes, as well as celebration cakes and classic afternoon teas. Only top quality ingredients including free range eggs, real butter and local ales are used in their delicious, high quality creations.

17

Brunswick Yard

EDITOR'S PICKS | FOR MORE INFO, SEE P111 |

The Brunswick Yard is a salvage yard and oriental carpet specialist where all sorts of goods can be found. They sell a selection of antique furniture, architectural salvage items, garden furniture, lights, decorative items and books.

18

The Rum Story

EDITOR'S PICKS | FOR MORE INFO, SEE P156

The Rum Story is a museum in Whitehaven set in the original 1785 rum shop and which takes you on an interactive journey through the history of the spirit. They have wonderful themed rooms filled with surprises throughout; the rooms include a rainforest, an African village, a slave ship, and a Coopers workshop

19

Stott Park Bobbin Mill

EDITOR'S PICKS | FOR MORE INFO, SEE P14 |

Stott Park Bobbin Mill achieved Silver in the Small Visitor Attraction of the Year Category at the Enjoy England Awards and Gold at the Cumbria Tourism Awards. Historically this extensive working mill produced millions of wooden bobbins vital to Lancashire's spinning and weaving industries. Today it is still a working bobbin mill.

20

CHAPTER TWO

OUT &
ABOUT

Coniston

OUT & ABOUT | CONISTON | LA21 8DU

Coniston was historically famous for its ore and slate mining. During Victorian times, the Furness Railway terminated in Coniston which opened up tourism to this beautiful area. Today hill-walking, rock-climbing and boating are popular pursuits from the village base.

Coniston offers a range of hotels, pubs and restaurants for those visiting the area. Grizedale Forest and Furness Fells offer walkers rugged and scenic countryside with majestic viewpoints. Tarn Hows (Tarn meaning lake), situated just a couple of miles away is a popular and beautiful spot for families to visit.

ADDRESS

1 Yewdale Road
LA21 8DU

PHONE

015394 41335

NEAR HERE

Waterhead Hotel (p49)

Chesters (p63)

The Little Ice Cream Shop (p152)

Haverthwaite Station

OUT & ABOUT | HAVERTHWAITE | LA12 8AL

Visit a bygone age by climbing aboard a steam train at Haverthwaite Station and enjoy the stunning views across Lake Windermere. The Furness Railway was developed during the 1850's and 1860's, at the height of the Industrial Revolution, to transport coal and iron ore from the coastal mines to the heavy industries of the North West and North East of England.

The station provides information on the fascinating history of the railway, and a fine collection of beautiful locomotives and rolling stock. It includes a shop, restaurant, playground and an engine shed, where a fine collection of locomotives are on display.

ADDRESS
Haverthwaite Station
LA12 8AL

PHONE
015395 31594

NEAR HERE
Old Hall Farm (p13)
WRS Architectural Antiques (p115)
Lakeland Motor Museum (p157)

Ruskin's View

OUT & ABOUT | **CARNFORTH** | **LA6 2BB**

The breathtaking panorama of the Lune Valley and Underley Hall can be seen from Ruskin's View. Painted by the celebrated artist JMW Turner in 1822. The 19th century art critic John Ruskin described the painting and scene as 'one of the loveliest views in England, therefore in the world'.

Climb the 86 'Radical Steps', rising from the riverside to St. Mary's churchyard, built in 1819 by local man Francis Pearson. At the top, this renowned scenic point and dramatic wide sweep of river towards the Middleton, Barbon and Leck Fells is the revered 'Ruskin's View'.

ADDRESS

Kirkby Lonsdale
LA6 2BB

PHONE

Not available

NEAR HERE

The Sun Inn (p52)

Lunesdale Bakery & Tearoom (p92)

Kirkby Lonsdale Brewery (p42)

Old Hall Farm

OUT & ABOUT | BOUTH | LA12 8JA

Set in idyllic surroundings, Old Hall Farm is a great day out for the family. This working farm is run according to authentic 19th century methods, with horse power and early vintage tractors used to work the fields. They aim to retain the old techniques and the farm is almost self-sufficient in terms of feed and stock rearing.

Milk from the farm's well cared for Jersey herd is used to make the ice cream and cream teas for its own tea room. Seasonal produce is sold in the farm's shop. The experience of watching the impressive shire horses at work, steam rollers and other nostalgic marvels, is an unforgettable one.

ADDRESS

Old Hall Farm
LA12 8JA

PHONE

01229 861993

NEAR HERE

Haverwaithe Station (p11)

Lakeland Motor Museum (p157)

Stott Park Bobbin Mill (p14)

Stott Park Bobbin Mill

OUT & ABOUT | **ULVERSTON** | **LA12 8AX**

Stott Park Bobbin Mill achieved Silver in the Small Visitor Attraction of the Year Category at the Enjoy England Awards and Gold at the Cumbria Tourism Awards. Historically this extensive working mill produced millions of wooden bobbins vital to Lancashire's spinning and weaving industries. Today it is still a working bobbin mill.

Tours and an exhibition bring to life the history of this industry with a family trail and dressing up for children, helping visitors understand what working at the mill would have been like and the difficult conditions workers faced at Stott Park Bobbin Mill.

ADDRESS
Finsthwaite
LA12 8AX

PHONE
01539 531087

NEAR HERE
Lakeland Motor Museum (p157)
Old Hall Farm (p13)
Haverwaithe Station (p11)

Ambleside

OUT & ABOUT | AMBLESIDE | LA22 9AN

Ambleside has a rich Roman history, with a fort named Galava, dating from AD79 and situated just south of the town. Today it serves as a base for those exploring the surrounding countryside and is particularly popular with climbers, hikers and mountain bikers.

Situated at the head of Lake Windemere, England's largest natural lake, Ambleside offers pubs, hotels, restaurants and shops, as well as boat trips across the water to soak up the mesmerising views. The outdoor interests of those that visit Ambleside is evident in the multitude of shops catering to climbing and biking needs.

ADDRESS

1-3 Rydal Road
LA22 9AN

PHONE

Not available

NEAR HERE

Push Cartel (p116)

Rattle Gill Café (p96)

Copper Pot (p80)

Grasmere

OUT & ABOUT | GRASMERE | LA22 9SY

Situated in the centre of the Lake District, Grasmere is best known for its famous resident, the poet William Wordsworth who described it as "the loveliest spot that man hath ever found." Its enchanting beauty attracts visitors from all over the world. Today the town is a tourist destination and offers a wide range of gift shops, cafés and accommodation.

The captivating countryside which surrounds Grasmere includes fells and mountains, lush woodland and tranquil lakes. Poets, writers and painters have been inspired by this stunning landscape for generations and it only takes one visit to see why.

ADDRESS
Broadgate House
LA22 9SY

PHONE
Not available

NEAR HERE
Grasmere Gingerbread (p138)
Heaton Cooper Studio (p167)
The Jumble Room (p74)

Cartmel

OUT & ABOUT | **CARTMEL** | **LA11 6QB**

The South Lakeland District fells and countryside surround Cartmel and its famous 12th Century medieval Priory Church offers centuries of enthralling history. The village itself offers great food and dining opportunities from artisan bread and cheese shops to traditional pubs.

Rich in culture and heritage, Cartmel is full of 16th-18th century buildings and the pretty river Eea streams through the village in a picturesque fashion. The village has become a haven for food lovers, from the village store's award-winning 'sticky toffee pudding' to the nationally acclaimed, Michelin starred restaurant L'Enclume.

ADDRESS
The Square, Cavendish Street
LA11 6QB

PHONE
Not available

NEAR HERE
Rogan & Company (p66)
Cartmel Priory (p170)
The Hazelmere (p85)

Kirkby Lonsdale

OUT & ABOUT | **CARNFORTH** | **LA6 2AE**

Kirkby Lonsdale is situated on the river Lune and on the edge of the Yorkshire Dales. Popular with walkers and cyclists, the Three Peaks are close by, making it an appealing base for those touring the area. This scenic small town is full of stone-built houses and plenty of respected restaurants, pubs and hotels.

Close to the spectacular Ingleton Falls and many lush, woodland trails, Kirky Lonsdale and the surrounding Lune Valley offer a stunning and diverse landscape for walkers and visitors. The town presents many quality, independent boutiques.

ADDRESS

Kirkby Lonsdale
LA6 2AE

PHONE

Not available

NEAR HERE

Ruskin's View (p12)

Kirkby Lonsdale Brewery (p42)

The Sun Inn (p52)

St. Bees

OUT & ABOUT | ST BEES | CA27 0ET

St Bees is well-known for its Norman Priory dating from 1120 and for being the starting point of the Wainwright "Coast to Coast" Walk. Just 50 miles South of the Scottish Border, this coastal town has a large sandy beach and has been a popular tourist destination for 150 years.

St Bees Head, a scenic headland close to the village, is a RSPB reserve and notable section of the Heritage Coast. The area of sea off the headland is part of the Cumbria Coast Marine Conservation Zone. Coastal paths in this area give awe-inspiring views of the Irish Sea.

ADDRESS
Seafront
CA27 0ET

PHONE
Not available

NEAR HERE
The Rum Story (p156)
Muncaster Castle (p172)
Ravenglass Station (p30)

Bassenthwaite Lake

OUT & ABOUT | KESWICK | CA13 9YD

Bassenthwaite Lake is one of the largest lakes in this region. Owned by the National Park Authority, the lake remains unspoilt with very little development on its shores. A small open-air theatre was built here in 1974, where it is thought that the poet Tennyson composed much of his poem 'Morte D'Arthur'.

Bassenthwaite Lake is a popular spot for sailing, with a boat club situated on its banks. A lakeside path on the western side offers beautiful views over the shimmering water. A wetland nature reserve is situated in the northern region of the lake, which is known for its rare birds and fish.

ADDRESS
Lakeside
CA13 9YD

PHONE
Not available

NEAR HERE
The Pheasant (p39)
The Lakes Distillery (p31)
The Moon & Sixpence (p79)

Buttermere

OUT & ABOUT | COCKERMOUTH | CA13 9XA

Buttermere is surrounded by vertiginous mountains and tranquil countryside. The path that runs the perimeter of Buttermere Lake can be completed within two to three hours and is popular with families. Owned by The National Trust, Buttermere Lake is renowned for its natural beauty and its name means 'lake by the dairy pastures'.

Buttermere Lake offers true serenity. With just a few farms and a couple of inns and cafés, the area remains rural and picturesque. Nearby, Syke Farm has a tearoom and is known for its homemade ice cream, made from the milk of its own herd of Ayrshire cattle.

ADDRESS
Buttermere
CA13 9XA

PHONE
Not available

NEAR HERE
Crummock Water (p24)
The Fish Inn (p58)
Skye Farm Tearoom (p99)

Crummock Water

OUT & ABOUT | COCKERMOUTH | CA13 9UY

Walking from the car park, the woodland dramatically opens up with incredible views of Crummock Water and over Grasmor, Rannerdale Knotts, Mellbreak and Red Pike. Wild swimming is popular in this lake and the more adventurous can take the (at times challenging) nine mile walk around the lake.

During bluebell season, the valley is illuminated in a magical purple-blue haze. Across Crummock is Scale Force, the tallest single drop waterfall in the Lake District with a height of 170 feet. Several paths lead up to the waterfall. The walk there and back from Buttermere car park is around two hours.

ADDRESS
B5289
CA13 9UY

PHONE
Not available

NEAR HERE
Buttermere (p23)
Skye Farm Tearoom (p99)
Honister Slate Mine (p113)

Derwentwater

OUT & ABOUT | KESWICK | CA12 5UP

Derwentwater is where the 2016 movie Swallows and Amazons was filmed. The natural beauty and wild landscape reinforces why the original books were inspired by these enchanting surroundings. Four islands are situated in Derwentwater and canoes can be hired to create your own adventure around the lake.

The islands in Derwentwater are cared for by the National Trust and the largest, named St Herbert's, was the inspiration for the fictional Owl Island in Beatrix Potter's 'The Tale of Squirrel Nutkin'. Diverse flora and fauna inhabit the lake, so certain areas are naturally protected with no-paddle zones.

ADDRESS

Borrowdale
CA12 5UP

PHONE

Not available

NEAR HERE

Lingholm Kitchen (p62)

Theatre by the Lake (p164)

Kong Adventure (p37)

Kirkstone Pass

OUT & ABOUT | WINDERMERE | LA23 1PS

Kirkstone Pass has an altitude of 1,489 feet and is the Lake District's highest pass open to cars, connecting Ambleside in the Rothay Valley to Patterdale in the Ullswater valley. There are many scenic viewpoints along the pass and the 500 year old Kirkstone Pass Inn, reportedly the third highest inn in England, stands close to the summit.

Near to the top of the Kirkstone Pass is the old Kirkstone Quarry where rock extraction took place to mine slate. Today cyclists and runners attempt the steep gradient of the pass which has been used for hundreds of years by farming families and travellers.

ADDRESS

Kirkstone Pass
LA23 1PS

PHONE

Not available

NEAR HERE

Ambleside (p15)

Mr H Tearoom (p84)

Beer (p147)

Rydal Water

OUT & ABOUT | AMBLESIDE | LA22 9LW

Wordsworth's Seat at Rydal Water was reportedly the romantic poet's favourite viewpoint in the Lake District. Rydal Water is the smallest lake in the region at just 3/4 mile long and 1/4 mile wide. The landscape around the lake is fascinating and Rydal Cave, a dramatic man-made cavern in the hill above the lake, provided slate over two hundred years ago to local villagers.

Both Dove Cottage and Rydal Mount, two of Wordworth's homes by the lakeside, can be seen from Rydal Water. Dove cottage today is a museum to Wordsworth and remains relatively untouched since his time there in the early 1800s.

ADDRESS
Ambleside
LA22 9LW

PHONE
Not available

NEAR HERE
The Red Gecko (p124)
Ambleside (p15)
The Jumble Room (p74)

Ravenglass Station

OUT & ABOUT | RAVENGLASS | CA18 1SW

The Ravenglass and Eskdale Railway is one of the oldest and longest narrow gauge railways in England. The heritage steam engines still transport passengers through scenically stunning scenery from Ravenglass, the only coastal village in the Lake District National Park to Dalegarth for Boot station.

This journey was one of Wainwright's favourites; crossing through seven miles of spectacular scenery within sight of the Scaféll Range mountains. The journey takes 40 minutes up the line from the protected nature reserves of the Ravenglass Estuary through ancient woodlands to the fells of the Eskdale Valley.

ADDRESS
Ravenglass & Eskdale Railway
CA18 1SW

PHONE
01229 717171

NEAR HERE
Mucaster Castle (p172)
The Byre Tea Rooms (p83)
St Bees (p21)

The Lakes Distillery

OUT & ABOUT | NEAR BASSENTHWAITE LAKE | CA13 9SJ

The vision of The Lakes Distillery is to create one of the leading malt spirits in the world, alongside one of the most unique visitor experiences in the Lake District. Located in a converted Victorian cattle farm, the creation of this world-class production facility of quality spirits was a labour of love.

Close to Bassenthwaite Lake and its majestic scenery, The Lakes Distillery is a driving force behind a revolution of 'new world' whisky distilleries. Their signature spirit, the Lakes Malt, will be released in 2018 however their gin and vodka brands are already making an impact.

ADDRESS

Setmurthy
CA13 9SJ

PHONE

017687 88850

NEAR HERE

Bassenthwaite Lake (p22)

The New Bookshop (p118)

The Pheasant (p39)

Hawkshead Brewery

OUT & ABOUT | KENDAL | LA8 9LR

Hawkshead Brewery is a small-scale brewery that is passionate about beer. Since 2002 it has been brewing traditional English beer with a contemporary twist. The processes are hands-on, with little automation, and the brewers hand-source all their hops to create brews that are pretty special.

Hawkshead Brewery's award-winning beer hall showcases every beer they produce and is an ideal spot for a long lunch, a relaxing tasting or simply to enjoy the regular live music sessions. Here you can try the great range of beers, from the core Lakeland range and the specials to the sought-after limited editions.

ADDRESS

Back Lane
LA8 9LR

PHONE

01539 822644

NEAR HERE

Plumgarths Farm Shop (p153)

Farrer's of Kendal (p95)

The Factory Tap (p40)

Brougham Castle

OUT & ABOUT | PENRITH | CA10 2AA

Dating back to the 13th century, the imposing ruins of Brougham Castle are situated near the picturesque crossing of the River Eamont in Cumbria. Known by its impressive double gatehouse and tower, the castle is an impressive and historically rich English Heritage site.

Built as a protective barrier against Scots invaders and as a respected residence, Brougham Castle fell into disrepair in the 1600s. However, even in its dilapidated condition, it remains an impressive landmark on the river Eamont. Panoramic views over the Eden Valley can be seen from the top of the castle's keep.

ADDRESS

Moor Lane
CA10 2AA

PHONE

01768 862488

NEAR HERE

Brunswick Yard (p111)

The Yard Kitchen (p107)

Langwathby Station Café (p106)

Bowness-on-Windermere

OUT & ABOUT | **WINDERMERE** | **LA23 3HQ**

Situated on the shore of Lake Windermere, Bowness-on-Windermere is one of the most popular tourist destinations in the Lake District due to it being a centre for outdoor and adventure activities. From a humble fishing village to a vibrant tourist destination, a number of the hotels today have been converted from large Victorian residences.

The Lake District's spectacular beauty and abundant wildlife inspired Beatrix Potter to write her much-loved stories. At Bowness-on-Windermere her tales are brought to life in the interactive 'World of Beatrix Potter,' a museum dedicated to the author.

ADDRESS

Bowness-on-Windermere
LA23 3HQ

PHONE

NEAR HERE

Blackwell, The Arts & Crafts House (p163)

La Gallerie D'Art (p114)

The Crafty Baa (p45)

Ford Park

OUT & ABOUT | **ULVERSTON** | **LA12 7JP**

Ford Park is a nine-acre green space with open fields, woodland and mature gardens surrounding the Grade II listed buildings situated in Ulverston. The space is ideal if you need to give the kids a bit of a run around. Activities include a nature trail, zip wires and orienteering through the woodland.

Ford Park is also an ideal starting point to see the Sir John Barrow Monument, a 100ft high lighthouse built to honour a famous son of Ulverston. Be sure to reward yourself with a pastry or pork pie afterwards at the on site Kitchen Garden and Café.

ADDRESS

Road Park
LA12 7JP

PHONE

01229 580666

NEAR HERE

Bici Café (p71)

Gillam's Tearoom (p65)

Squirrel (p129)

Keswick Launch

OUT & ABOUT | **LAKESIDE** | **CA12 5DJ**

Keswick Launch Co. offers lake cruises to experience the natural beauty of Derwentwater, with staggering views of the surrounding fells. The four launches have open and covered decks and operate on a regular timetable throughout the year. You can also explore the lake at your own pace on one of their rowing boats.

Take the 50 minute round boat trip with Keswick Launch Co. or disembark at one of their eight jetties en-route, to discover famous landmarks such as Ashness Bridge, Lodore Falls and Lingholm, the holiday home of Beatrix Potter.

ADDRESS
The Waters Edge
CA12 5DJ

PHONE
Unavailable

NEAR HERE
Theatre by the Lake (p164)

Lingholm Kitchen (p62)

Fellpack (p67)

Kong Adventure

OUT & ABOUT | KESWICK | CA12 5EZ

Kong Adventure is home to a selection of exciting indoor and outdoor activities, perfect for thrill seekers and climbers. Inside the shop on-site they stock the very best climbing gear and outdoor clothing as well as other useful accessories and footwear.

Kong Adventure has one of the UK's only Ice climbing walls in their sealed -7c room and a large indoor climbing wall, indoor caving and soft play area. Off-site activities include outdoor climbing, climb and mine, via ferrata, Ghyll scrambling and more. Their site in Keswick is ideal for wet weather excitement and is good for all ages and abilities.

ADDRESS

Heads Lane

CA12 5EZ

PHONE

017687 75907

NEAR HERE

Morrels (p90)

Jasper's (p101)

Derwentwater (p25)

CHAPTER THREE
PUBLIC
HOUSES

The Pheasant

PUBLIC HOUSE | COCKERMOUTH | CA13 9YE

The Pheasant in Bassenthwaite is stylistically stuck in a bit of a time warp but the quality of food and service remains popular today. Using a number of local ingredients in their dishes, you can choose to eat in the slightly more formal Fell Restaurant or in the relaxed bistro.

Surrounded by the beautiful scenery of Lake Bassenthwaite, this 17th century coaching inn is a good stop off for walkers and dogs are also welcomed. The pub garden offers limited seating but a pretty environment to have a drink on warmer days. The characterful and traditional bar area is a cozy place to sit with a glass of wine.

ADDRESS
Bassenthwaite Lake
CA13 9YE

PHONE
017687 76234

NEAR HERE
The Lakes Distillery (p31)
Bassenthwaite Lake (p22)
Derwent Pencil Museum (p168)

The Factory Tap

PUBLIC HOUSE | KENDAL | LA9 7DE

The Factory Tap claims to be Kendal's premier real ale pub and a location for discovering new hand-crafted beers. Genuine hospitality is key to their ethos and they also carry a selection of quality wines. Pro-active at hosting live music sessions and supporting local art festivals, the pub is at the heart of the community.

The Factory Tap is a contemporary pub set within an old stone building. At the end of each month they bring the culinary delights of street food to the pub and have showcased local foodies' creations; from burgers, fish and chips and Caribbean to Thai, pizzas and vegan friendly offerings.

ADDRESS
5 Aynam Road
LA9 7DE

PHONE
015394 82541

NEAR HERE
Comida Food (p72)

The Moon (p73)

Baba Ganoush (p144)

The Dalesman Inn

PUBLIC HOUSE | SEDBERGH | LA10 5BN

The Dalesman Inn is a fully refurbished, contemporary Free House. With an emphasis on quality, the restaurant menu changes with the seasons and the food is locally sourced. A great base for the Lakes and the Dales, the Dalesman is in the heart of walking country and their homemade ice cream is a welcome treat in the warmer months.

This family-run inn is proud to source its key ingredients locally, with their lamb coming from Hebblethwaite, less than two miles away. The pub is a great place to end up after a riverside walk, with their woodburner and characterful stone walls creating a cozy atmosphere.

ADDRESS

Main Street
LA10 5BN

PHONE

015396 21183

NEAR HERE

Fairfield Mill (p162)

Three Hares (p94)

The Dalesman Inn (p41)

Kirkby Lonsdale Brewery

PUBLIC HOUSE | KIRKBY | LA6 2AB

Kirkby Lonsdale Brewery Co Ltd was established in 2009. Brewing has been at the heart of the town for centuries until the trade had all but died out. The company owners' passion for real ale led to the re-establishment of a local brewery and their pub called The Royal Barn. Situated at the Old Station Yard, the brewery has opened its own beer barn in Kirkby Lonsdale.

The first beer produced by Kirkby Lonsdale Brewery is "Ruskins," named after the iconic Ruskin's View, which Turner famously painted in 1816. The brewery pump clips are branded with an image of local landmark, Devils Bridge and all of their beer names are linked to the local area.

ADDRESS

New Road
LA6 2AB

PHONE

015242 71918

NEAR HERE

The Plough (p44)

The Sun Inn (p52)

Lunesdale Bakery & Tearoom (p92)

The Strickland Arms

PUBLIC HOUSE | KENDAL | LA8 8DZ

Located on the edge of the Lake District, overlooking the entrance to historic Sizergh Castle near Kendal, lies the pub The Strickland Arms. Its interior incorporates light to inky green walls and traditional portraiture and paintings wth an equestrian theme, worn wooden and stone floors with large rugs and grand fireplaces with roaring fires.

The pub itself is traditional in ambience and its menu offers everything from sandwiches and steak to fish pie and fish and chips. The Strickland Arms uses local ingredients where possible. The relaxed and homely environment is great for families and dogs are also welcomed.

ADDRESS

Sizergh
LA8 8DZ

PHONE

015395 61010

NEAR HERE

Low Sizergh Barn (p134)

Hare and Hounds (p51)

The Punch Bowl (p53)

The Plough

PUBLIC HOUSE | LUPTON | LA6 1PJ

The Plough near Kirkby Lonsdale is a tastefully styled, contemporary restaurant and hotel situated inside a characterful old coaching inn. With beautiful original beams set against freshly painted walls and a neutral colour palette, the quality and attention to detail offers a little luxury in the countryside.

Roaring woodburners add to the relaxing ambience at The Plough and the menu offers quality British cuisine, with the meat and other specific ingredients sourced locally. The bedrooms offer superb accommodation with large bathrooms, roll top baths and some luxurious furnishings.

ADDRESS

Cow Brow
LA6 1PJ

PHONE

015395 67700

NEAR HERE

Kitridding Farm Shop (p154)

The Strickland Arms (p43)

Low Sizergh Barn (p134)

The Crafty Baa

PUBLIC HOUSE | WINDERMERE | LA23 1AB

If you enjoy craft beer The Crafty Baa offers over 50 varieties, with wine and cider also available for you to choose from. Located in Windermere, charcuterie and cheese slates are also served in this relaxed family run business.

The Crafty Baa has a cozy open fire and plays a range of Motown, Jazz, Blues and Soul whilst you relax with friends. Acoustic sets are often played here in this rustic setting. Tucked away in Windermere, this little bar is strewn with fairy lights and has a welcoming vibe.

ADDRESS

21 Victoria Street
LA23 1AB

PHONE

015394 88002

NEAR HERE

The Pig (p91)

Agnes & Cat (p112)

Waterhead Coffee (p64)

Wateredge Inn

PUBLIC HOUSE | AMBLESIDE | LA22 0EP

The Wateredge Inn has an enviable location right on the shores of beautiful Lake Windermere. Its mesmerising setting offers those wanting to drink or dine, the perfect view, with boats and water steamers cruising by. Wildlife is abundant too and can often be seen from this spectacular spot.

From the lakeside terrace to the cozy fireside, The Wateredge Inn is a scenic place to have a drink, whatever the season. The interior is simple and traditional and its menu offers lots of pub classics. However, it really is the breathtaking location that people come to enjoy here.

ADDRESS

Borrans Road

LA22 0EP

PHONE

015394 32332

NEAR HERE

Waterhead Coffee (p64)

Bowness-on-Windermere (p34)

Chesters (p63)

The Waterhead

PUBLIC HOUSE | AMBLESIDE | LA22 0ER

The Waterhead Hotel is yet another fantastic business situated in this beautiful area of the Lake District. Its rustic stone exterior sits amongst immaculate gardens and rolling hills and its riverside location is unbeatable.

The Waterhead Hotel has a simple, contemporary style and guests can stay in one of their rooms which are modern and furnished with comfort in mind. The conservatory dining room allows for panoramic views across Lake Windermere, where guests can indulge in dishes such as seared king scallops and roast Cumbrian lamb.

ADDRESS

Lake Road
LA22 0ER

PHONE

015394 32566

NEAR HERE

Copper Pot (p80)

Cathedral Cavern (p169)

The Crafty Baa (p45)

The Cavendish Arms

PUBLIC HOUSE | CARTMEL | LA11 6QA

This 450 year old coaching inn is situated in the picturesque village of Cartmel. The Cavendish Arms offers character and charm with a roaring fire and original oak beams. There is a classic pub menu using some local produce with dishes including fish pie and mixed platters for sharing.

Offering stunning views of the South Lakeland District fells and countryside, Cartmel has developed around its 12th Century medieval Priory Church and The Cavendish Arms is at its heart. This medieval village is surrounded by stunning landscape that meets with the sands of Morecambe Bay on the edge of the Furness Peninsula.

ADDRESS

Cavendish Street
LA11 6QA

PHONE

015395 36240

NEAR HERE

Cartmel Cheeses (p133)

Hot Wines (p135)

Rogan & Company (p66)

Hare and Hounds

PUBLIC HOUSE | KENDAL | LA8 8PN

The Hare and Hounds is situated in a perfect position for visiting the Lake District and is a fully refurbished coaching inn dating back to the 17th century. They provide great home-inspired meals, using local ingredients where possible. The black slate floors and open fire, create a cosy and convivial atmosphere.

Much like the styling of the pub and restaurant below, the comfy rooms are a fusion of Victorian and contemporary design. The Hare and Hounds nestles in stunning surroundings and is a welcome place to rejuvenate after a day of walking or being outdoors.

ADDRESS
Levens
LA8 8PN

PHONE
015395 60004

NEAR HERE
The Strickland Arms (p43)
Low Sizergh Barn (p134)
The Plough (p44)

The Sun Inn

PUBLIC HOUSE | KIRKBY LONSDALE | LA6 2AU

The Sun Inn in Kirkby Lonsdale is a 17th century inn well known for its fine, seasonal menu and wine tastings. It combines tradition and charm with modern and stylish design. In a fantastic location where three counties meet, it is within easy access of the Dales, the Lakes and the Trough of Bowland.

Behind The Sun Inn is the original sundial which inspires its name. The river Lune is situated nearby and provides a renowned beauty spot. The inn has 13 rooms, all designed with comfort in mind. From the wood burners to the old stone interior walls, The Sun Inn offers a characterful place to enjoy a meal or stay.

ADDRESS
6 Market Street
LA6 2AU

PHONE
015242 71965

NEAR HERE
The Plough (p44)
The Crossing Point Café (p105)
Ruskin's View (p12)

The Punch Bowl

PUBLIC HOUSE | LYTH VALLEY | LA8 8HR

The Punch Bowl is situated in the heart of the unspoilt Lyth Valley at Crosthwaite in Cumbria. Offering a 'unique blend of old and new,' The Punch Bowl is a luxurious country restaurant offering quality dining and stylish accommodation. Flickering fires, oak beams and polished oak floors only enhance the ambience.

The Punch Bowl's tasteful country decor is stylish yet welcoming, with deep leather sofas and armchairs, stone fireplaces and lots of candlelight. The menu at the Punch Bowl is traditional and sophisticated, presented with flair and with a focus on local and seasonal produce.

ADDRESS

Crosthwaite
LA8 8HR

PHONE

015395 68237

NEAR HERE

Blackwell, The Arts & Crafts House (p163)

Hawkshead Brewery (p32)

Plumgarths Farm Shop (p153)

The Bitter End

PUBLIC HOUSE | COCKERMOUTH | CA13 9PJ

The Bitter End is a traditional pub and restaurant in Cockermouth which is popular with the locals and often busy. Well positioned in this market town, the pub serves a classic menu and changes their specials weekly. Home to one of the smallest breweries in Cumbria, the pub has a good range of real ales and beers alongside wines and an extensive gin menu.

The interior of The Bitter End pub is also traditional with a brick fireplace and woodburner, stone, wood and carpeted floors, a dark wooden bar and comfortable furnishings. This is a dog friendly pub and food here is considered good value.

ADDRESS

15 Kirkgate
CA13 9PJ

PHONE

01900 828993

NEAR HERE

Merienda (p81)

Sarah's (p98)

The New Bookshop (p118)

The Fat Lamb

PUBLIC HOUSE | KIRKBY STEPHEN | CA17 4LL

Situated near Kirkby Stephen, The Fat Lamb is a rustic inn which is well situated between the Yorkshire Dales and the Lake District, making the most of the surrounding areas of natural beauty. The Fat Lamb has earned itself a reputation for its good food, using fresh, locally sourced produce in their home-cooked dishes.

The interior of the Fat Lamb is old-fashioned with traditional furnishings, carpeted and wooden flooring and roaring fires. Situated just off the road, views of the beautiful rolling hills can be seen from the pretty pub garden.

ADDRESS

Crossbank, Ravenstonedale
CA17 4LL

PHONE

015396 23242

NEAR HERE

Buttercup (p119)

Brough Castle (p161)

Fairfield Mill (p162)

Fish Inn

PUBLIC HOUSE | **COCKERMOUTH** | **CA13 9XA**

The Fish Inn is situated next to Buttermere Lake and surrounded by the mesmerising beauty of the hills and water. Just five minutes walk from Buttermere and Crummock Water at the foot of Honister Pass, the inn is full of charm and character. Historically, this was the home of Mary Robinson (The Maid of Buttermere).

Passionate about ales, The Fish Inn sells a great selection of locally produced varieties. It is the location of the pub which attracts visitors, many of whom are walkers, soaking up the awe-inspiring beauty of the area. The menu is classic and the interior is basic and quite old-fashioned.

ADDRESS
Buttermere
CA13 9XA

PHONE
017687 70253

NEAR HERE
Skye Farm Tearoom (p99)
Honister Slate Mine (p113)
Grange Café (p97)

The Highwayman

PUBLIC HOUSE | KIRKBY LONSDALE | LA6 2RJ

The Highwayman is celebrated for its culinary excellence. The garden terrace is a beautiful spot for al fresco dining during the Summer, whilst glowing log fires inside make it a cozy destination during the Winter. The Highwayman is considered an iconic gastro haven for all seasons.

The Highwayman is situated just in Lancashire and a stone's throw from the borders of Yorkshire and Cumbria. The head chef showcases the three counties "food heroes" by incorporating the very best local suppliers' ingredients into his masterpieces. This is a destination pub where food quality and provenance are a top priority.

ADDRESS

Nether Burrow
LA6 2RJ

PHONE

015242 73338

NEAR HERE

Lancaster Castle (p166)

Ruskins View (p12)

The Fenwick Arms (p60)

Fenwick Arms

PUBLIC HOUSE | CLAUGHTON | LA2 9LA

The beautiful Fenwick Arms is over 250 years old and exudes historic and atmospheric charm. The stylish interior cleverly incorporates the beautiful features of the old building, with its stone walls, large open fires and oak floors into a luxurious, country chic aesthetic.

Sensational seafood specials are delivered with exceptional quality at The Fenwick Arms. Daily changing specials reflect the seasonality of the menu and feature the catch of the day, straight from celebrated fishmonger Chris Neve at Fleetwood fishing port. The nine contemporary guest rooms are well appointed and elegant.

ADDRESS

Lancaster Road
LA2 9LA

PHONE

015242 21157

NEAR HERE

The Highwayman (p59)

The Plough (p44)

Ruskin's View (p12)

CHAPTER FOUR

PLACES
TO EAT

Lingholm Kitchen

PLACES TO EAT | KESWICK | CA12 5TZ

The octagonal walled garden sits on the same spot as the old Lingholm Kitchen gardens which Beatrix Potter credited as her inspiration for Mr McGregor's garden in The Tale of Peter Rabbit. Built in a Victorian style, the garden has herbaceous borders while central areas are reserved for vegetables which are then served fresh in the Kitchen.

Lingholm Kitchen aims to offer the best day time eating experience in the area. Its emphasis on food provenance can be seen on their boards, where they list the farms and suppliers of their local meat and dairy produce. Local and seasonal ingredients are a focus.

ADDRESS

Lingholm Lodge
CA12 5TZ

PHONE

017687 71206

NEAR HERE

Theatre by the Lake (p164)

Derwent Pencil Museum (p168)

The Square Orange Café (p109)

Chesters by the River

PLACES TO EAT | **AMBLESIDE** | **LA22 9NJ**

Chesters by the River is situated in an enviable position with a deck overlooking the River Brathay. With a counter brimming with some of the finest looking cakes and brownies we ever did see, this contemporary restaurant offers rainbow salads and pizzas and flatbreads from its wood fired oven.

While the counter is covered with some quick to order dishes like frittatas and sausage rolls. The combination of its riverside position and delicious food makes this a popular choice in Ambleside. Sit on the deck to eat and listen to the water cascading past, as the rays of the sun stream through the trees.

ADDRESS

Skelwith Bridge
LA22 9NJ

PHONE

015394 34711

NEAR HERE

Copper Pot (p80)

Wateredge Inn (p48)

Waterhead Coffee (p64)

Waterhead Coffee

PLACES TO EAT | AMBLESIDE | LA22 0EY

With mesmerising views of the lake, Waterhead Coffee in Ambleside offers one of the most scenic spots in the lakes for a coffee and something home-baked. Beautifully presented cakes are placed on slate boards and a pretty outside window on the terrace serves ice creams on warmer days.

Inside, views of the water are framed by the windows. The interior style is a contemporary take on shabby chic, with bunting, gingham, uplifting quotes and vibrant floral highlights. The home-baked blueberry scones with jam or scones with warm rum butter are examples of the indulgent treats on offer at Waterhead Coffee.

ADDRESS

Borrans Road
LA22 0EY

PHONE

015394 32038

NEAR HERE

Wateredge Inn (p48)

The Pig (p91)

Copper Pot (p80)

Gillam's Tea Room & Grocer

PLACES TO EAT | ULVERSTON | LA12 7LT

Gillam's Tea Room and Specialist grocer is an institution in Ulverston, with the Gillam family having provided fine food and excellent service in Ulverston since 1892, when John James Gillam opened his cash and wholesale grocers on Market Street. Today the tearoom offers wholesome home-cooked food made from local produce and the grocery sells organic fruit and vegetables, with an emphasis on provenance.

Gillam's has retained many of the store's original features and old-world charm; from its fireplace, high ceilings and tea-lined shelves to the quality of service and pretty store front.

ADDRESS

64 Market Street
LA12 7LT

PHONE

01229 587564

NEAR HERE

Squirrel (p129)

Bici Café (p71)

Tape Design (p128)

Rogan & Company

PLACES TO EAT | CARTMEL | LA11 6QD

Rogan & Company is the sister restaurant to Simon Rogan's nationally acclaimed L'Enclume. Rogan & Co offers a more casual dining experience while "retaining the unparalleled precision and creativity of Simon's distinctive culinary style, using exceptional Cumbrian, as well as home-grown, ingredients that are harvested in their prime."

Situated in a beautiful old stone building with large windows, beams and fireplaces, the restaurant is minimal and modern in style with pale walls, stripped wood floors and simple furnishings. The emphasis is on the quality of the food and its innovative composition and flavour.

ADDRESS

Devonshire Square
LA11 6QD

PHONE

015395 35917

NEAR HERE

Cartmel Priory (p170)

The Cavendish Arms (p50)

Hot Wines (p135)

Fellpack

PLACES TO EAT | **KESWICK** | **CA12 5BS**

Fellpack is 'the unique creation of a group of friends with a thirst for adventure and a love of great food'. Their ethos is to create delicious food from local ingredients whilst enjoyed in the comfort of their restaurant or taken away to enjoy in front of breathtaking views from a fell top, or one of the many beautiful lakes.

Fellpack's considered menu balances 'classic flavours with bold innovation.' Dishes are generally healthy and creative. The restaurant has a stylish and rustic aesthetic and serves delicious coffee alongside flapjacks and brownies, for those needing some extra hiking fuel.

ADDRESS
19 Lake Road
CA12 5BS

PHONE
017687 71177

NEAR HERE
Morrels (p90)
Theatre by the Lake (p164)
Lingholm Kitchen (p62)

The Bakery at No.4

PLACES TO EAT | KENDAL | LA9 4QB

Based in Kendal, The Bakery at No.4 specialises in making beautiful bespoke wedding cakes, as well as celebration cakes and classic afternoon teas. Only top quality ingredients including free range eggs, real butter and local ales are used in their delicious, high quality creations.

Seasonally led, The Bakery at No.4's menu is ever-changing whilst also featuring regular favourites. The bakery offers an array of delicious pastries, cakes and traybakes washed down with high quality teas and artisan coffee, in a relaxed, cozy, home-like environment.

ADDRESS
40 Woolpack Road
LA9 4QB

PHONE
07500 772134

NEAR HERE
Staff of Life (p145)
Abbot Hall Art Gallery (p160)
The Factory Tap (p40)

Bici Café

PLACES TO EAT | **ULVERSTON** | **LA12 7BJ**

Bici Café is a modern, authentic Italian café and Kitchen in Ulverston. With an industrial style, the café offers a daytime selection of brunch-style light bites and artisan baked savouries, whilst the evenings are all about their delicious wood-fired pizzas, Italian small plates, salami, cheese and a selection of Italian desserts.

Simplicity and quality are part of the success of Bici Café. With a menu of both traditional and contemporary pizzas, the dough is made using a "long-fermentation" method, adding to the taste and digestability. The ambience is buzzy and relaxed.

ADDRESS
1 The Gill
LA12 7BJ

PHONE
01229 581833

NEAR HERE
Gillam's Tea Room (p65)
Ford Park (p35)
Lakeland Motor Museum (p157)

Comida Food

PLACES TO EAT | KENDAL | LA9 4HE

Comida is a high quality Spanish tapas restaurant founded by a husband and wife team with Valencian heritage. The flavours from this region inspire the menu alongside classic Spanish dishes, from patatas bravas and paella to spanish omelette. Craft Spanish beer and wine accompany the considered and affordably priced menu.

The restaurant places an emphasis on casual eating in a relaxed and stylish atmosphere. The vibrant coloured, Spanish tiled bar with bar stools, exhibits homebaked cakes and pastries, illuminated by the pendant lighting hanging from above.

ADDRESS
90 Highgate
LA9 4HE

PHONE
Not available

NEAR HERE
Abbot Hall Art Gallery (p160)
1657 Chocolate House (p139)
Farrer's of Kendal (p95)

The Moon Highgate

PLACES TO EAT | KENDAL | LA9 4EN

The Moon Highgate in Kendal is a restaurant offering 'expertly prepared, high quality food in a comfortable, relaxed setting'. Head Chef and proprietor Leon Whitehead has created a contemporary British menu that changes with the seasons and is carefully crafted to make the most of the finest local ingredients.

Having travelled extensively through Africa, Spain and France, Leon has gleaned considerable knowledge and inspiration from restaurants and chefs throughout the world. He brings this expertise and creativity to The Moon Highgate where the design is modern and minimal and the cuisine speaks for itself.

ADDRESS

129 Highgate

LA9 4EN

PHONE

01539 729254

NEAR HERE

The Bakery at No.4 (p70)

Baba Ganoush (p144)

The Factory Tap (p40)

The Jumble Room

PLACES TO EAT | GRASMERE | LA22 9SU

The Jumble Room is a vibrant and intimate restaurant established over twenty years ago by the owners Andy and Chrissy who are passionate about food. The menu focuses on local and organic produce with Thai and Mediterranean accents. The food has gained a reputation for its excellence and the service is rather exceptional too.

The restaurant interior is scattered with large canvases of farm animals on scarlet red walls and an eclectic array of glass pendants and cutlery are suspended from the window. Mismatched pillows are scattered on the benches and candles light the restaurant at night.

ADDRESS
Langdale Road
LA22 9SU

PHONE
015394 35188

NEAR HERE
Lucia's (p100)
The Herdy Shop (p130)
Baldry's (p87)

Emma's Dell

PLACES TO EAT | AMBLESIDE | LA22 9SX

Emma's Dell is a family owned Crêperie in Grasmere, in the heart of the Lake District. Serving sweet and savoury crepes, homemade cakes, ice cream, artisan coffee, loose leaf-teas and alcohol, this light and airy Crêperie is contemporary in style.

Emma's Dell was inspired by a ski trip taken by Emma and her family and their love of their apres ski indulgences. Sumptuous and indulgent cakes in glass stands line the counter here, whilst a delicious array of homemade ice creams can be selected from the chalkboard menu. Ice creams range from Madagascan Vanilla and Gingerbread to vegan Coconut.

ADDRESS

Grasmere
LA22 9SX

PHONE

015394 35234

NEAR HERE

The Red Gecko (p124)

Grasmere Gingerbread Shop (p138)

The Jumble Room (p74)

Notes

Tried our app?

bestofengland.com/app

The Moon & Sixpence

PLACES TO EAT | COCKERMOUTH | CA13 9LE

The Moon and Sixpence is an artisanal coffee shop in Cockermouth which has built a strong reputation for its high quality coffee and home-baked pastries. The owner, Stephen Kidd, has immersed himself in coffee culture and even lived in one of the world's coffee capitals, Vancouver where he gleaned experience from the experts.

The Moon and Sixpence is a stylish coffeehouse with upcycling being a key component of its modern interior design.

White walls, chalkboards and the wooden furniture and counter keep the ambience calm and relaxed. This is a great spot for a lovingly made coffee.

ADDRESS

29 Main Street
CA13 9LE

PHONE

01900 829378

NEAR HERE

Merienda (p81)

The New Bookshop (p118)

The Bitter End (p56)

Copper Pot

PLACES TO EAT | AMBLESIDE | LA22 0BU

The Copper Pot café is family owned and one of the most popular in Ambleside. The interior showcases beautiful local materials, from the slate floors to the stone interior walls. With an indulgent array of sumptous cakes overspilling onto the wooden counter, the quality of food and attention to detail is becoming locally renowned.

The terrace at The Coffee Pot is the perfect spot for coffee or al fresco dining. Inside, a cozy fireplace makes for an idyllic place to sit after a walk on colder days. From homemade burgers and ciabattas to salad plates, the menu is dynamic and places an emphasis on quality.

ADDRESS

Church Street
LA22 0BU

PHONE

015394 31911

NEAR HERE

LilyLou's (p125)

Rattle Gill Café (p96)

Mr H Tearoom (p84)

Merienda

PLACES TO EAT | KESWICK | CA12 5JD

Merienda is an exceptionally stylish and contemporary licensed restaurant/café serving breakfast and brunch through to an eclectic evening menu. With a simple, globally influenced menu, the founders' aim has been to use wholesome, seasonal ingredients whilst drawing inspiration from around the world.

Exceptional ingredients are the focus at Merienda and they are serious about their coffee too, serving the delicious Monmouth brand. This is a sleek establishment with sophisticated design, from its light parquet flooring and creative pendant lighting to its artistic installation above the beautifully crafted bar.

ADDRESS
10 Main Street
CA12 5JD

PHONE
017687 72024

NEAR HERE
The Lakes Distillery (p31)
The Pheasant (p39)
The Bitter End (p56)

The Windmill Café

PLACES TO EAT | CALDBECK | CA7 8DR

The Watermill Café in Caldbeck specialises in delicious home-cooked food using only the finest local produce, served in the beautiful surroundings of a converted watermill. In warmer weather sit on the terrace with views over the river Caldbeck. During the winter months the restaurant is warmed by a cosy log stove and lit by candles.

The watermill was built by a Rector of Caldbeck in 1702 in a secluded position on the riverbank. From 1702 to 1933 it was used as a stone-grinding corn mill and today the original waterwheel has been restored and enhances the old-world charm of the café.

ADDRESS

Priest's Mill
CA7 8DR

PHONE

016974 78267

NEAR HERE

Half Moon Interiors (p126)

Bassenthwaite Lake (p22)

The Yard Kitchen (p107)

Byre Tea Room

PLACES TO EAT | MILLOM | LA19 5TJ

The Byre Tea Room in Bootle may often be overlooked due to its rather unattractive exterior but inside the barn beams and woodburner create a comfortable stop off in this beautiful area. The food is simple but hugely popular and their sweet afternoon tea platters are beautifully presented and generous.

The relaxed farm table style at the Byre Tea Room makes it a popular choice with families. Dishes are homemade, with lots of local ingredients used within everything from their roasts to their soups. There is also a farm and craft shop on site. With views over the fells, this is a great spot for casual eating.

ADDRESS

Millstones Barn, Bootle
LA19 5TJ

PHONE

01229 718757

NEAR HERE

Muncaster Castle (p172)

Ravenglass Station (p30)

Coniston (p10)

Mr H Tearoom

PLACES TO EAT | AMBLESIDE | LA22 0AD

Mr H's in Ambleside is a light and airy café with high ceilings, large windows and plenty of natural light. Serving teas, coffees, cakes and sandwiches, this is a casual spot with lovely views of the town. Cake stands with tiers of scones and home-baked indulgences are placed on the counter.

With vintage accessories and details highlighting the walls and shelves, the staff are friendly and the presentation is good. Conveniently located near to the bus stop, Mr H's Tearoom offers simple, tasty dishes in the heart of the town.

ADDRESS

Lake Road
LA22 0AD

PHONE

015394 31421

NEAR HERE

Chesters (p63)

Rydal Water (p29)

Kirkstone Pass (p28)

The Hazelmere

PLACES TO EAT | GRANGE-OVER-SANDS | LA11 6ED

The Hazelmere is an independent, family-run café and delicatessen in Grange-over-Sands. Community and environment are hugely important to The Hazelmere and they invest in both by supporting local suppliers and by making and baking on site.

The Hazelmere is passionate about serving local, seasonal food as evidenced in its quality and presentation. As connoisseurs of tea, the varieties available are extensive. The café is contemporary and the bakery bakes bread traditionally, from delicious farmhouse whites and spelt & honey to beetroot & apple. They also make over thirty different cakes fresh each day.

ADDRESS

2 Yewbarrow Terrace
LA11 6ED

PHONE

015395 32972

NEAR HERE

Fat Flour (p141)

Cartmel Priory (p170)

Rogan & Company (p66)

Lanercost Tea Room & Gift Shop

PLACES TO EAT | LANERCOST | CA8 2HQ

Lanercost Tea Room specialises in fresh, homemade food using quality local produce. The tea room is situated next door to the 12th century Lanercost Priory and a short walk from the World Heritage site of Hadrian's Wall. The wall dates back to 128 AD when it served as a defensive fortification in the Roman province of Britannia under the reign of emperor Hadrian.

There is also a gift shop on site selling locally made products including pure wool throws and decor items for the home. If you are looking to explore Hadrian's Wall then this makes an ideal starting point. Parking is free and dogs are welcome too.

ADDRESS
Brampton
CA8 2HQ

PHONE
016977 41267

NEAR HERE
Lanercost Priory (p173)
Carlisle Cathedral (p165)
Half Moon Interiors (p126)

Baldry's

PLACES TO EAT | **AMBLESIDE** | **LA22 9SP**

Baldry's is a vintage style tearoom located in the heart of Grasmere village and renowned for over 25 years for their home baking. Serving light lunches, loose leaf teas, fresh ground coffee and an array of mouth-watering home baked-cakes, this tearoom offers a refined environment.

Baldry's is not like your typical chintzy vintage tearoom, this establishment offers a simple but distinguished interior with large brass mirrors, chandeliers and a solid wood floor. Afternoon tea is served here and is popular. Ingredients used in their home-cooked food are locally sourced from reputable suppliers.

ADDRESS
Red Lion Square, Grasmere
LA22 9SP

PHONE
07760 773671

NEAR HERE
Rydal Water (p29)
Ambleside (p15)
The Jumble Room (p74)

Morrels

PLACES TO EAT | KESWICK | CA12 5DQ

Morrels is a popular choice with theatregoers due to its proximity to Keswick's Theatre By The Lake and its deliberate early opening time for pre-theatre dining. The restaurant is contemporary in style with high ceilings, light walls, stripped wood floors, high backed chairs and enormous arched windows which allow natural light to flood in.

The menu at Morrels is imaginative and highly regarded. Executive Head Chef Karl Link is one of the restaurant's founding partners and has tried to create a menu which appeals to a range of tastes and budgets. The menu changes regularly and on Sunday it serves roasts.

ADDRESS
34 Lake Road
CA12 5DQ

PHONE
017687 72666

NEAR HERE
Fellpack (p67)

The Square Orange Café (p109)

Theatre by the Lake (p164)

The Pig

PLACES TO EAT | WINDERMERE | LA23 1EA

The Pig in Windermere is a contemporary restaurant offering a classic British menu based on fresh local produce. Pork in all its forms is their specialty. From juicy ribs and their popular pig platter to smoked pig and a hog roast, which is cooked daily on the rotisserie, The Pig is a carnivore's paradise.

To wash down the hog, they stock a vast selection of local ales and wines. The Pig does have vegetarian options on the menu too. The interior of the restaurant is modern and casual with vibrant red walls, high tables, leather bar stools and a woodburner. Pig themed decorations feature strongly here.

ADDRESS

13 Crescent Road
LA23 1EA

PHONE

01539 234010

NEAR HERE

Bowness-on-Windermere (p34)

Blackwell, The Arts & Crafts House (p163)

Hawkshead Brewery (p32)

Lunesdale Bakery & Tea Room

PLACES TO EAT | KIRKBY LONSDALE | LA6 2AJ

This long-established, traditional bakery and tearoom has maintained its reputation over the years for its quality artisanal breads, pastries, cakes and savoury produce. The charm here is in its reputation and emphasis on its produce.

Next door to the bakery is their tearoom with a roaring fire and old-fashioned cozy ambience. Serving traditional food, the tearoom serves breakfasts and lunches in generous portions. Step back in time with a slower pace and style here at Kirkby Lonsdale's Lunesdale Bakery and Tearoom.

ADDRESS

50 Main Street
LA6 2AJ

PHONE

015242 71296

NEAR HERE

Parma Violet (p131)

Dales Traditional Butchers (p140)

The Sun Inn (p52)

Notes

Tried our app?

bestofengland.com/app

Three Hares

PLACES TO EAT | SEDBURGH | LA10 5AB

The Three Hares is a family run seasonal and locally sourced café, bistro and bakery situated in the book town of Sedbergh at the foot of the Howgills. The cooking style here is influenced by the founders heritage of both the wild food of the local area and growing up in Germany with Japanese parents.

The Three Hares offers an innovative menu with exceptionally high quality food. From breakfast and lunch through to dinner, this is a true gem of a restaurant in every respect from the passion of the co-founders and rustic, cozy restaurant ambience to the exquisite and highly considered dishes.

ADDRESS

57 Main Street
LA10 5AB

PHONE

015396 21058

NEAR HERE

The Dalesman Inn (p41)

Weaving Studio (p127)

No. 6 Finkle Street (p108)

Farrer's of Kendal

PLACES TO EAT | **KENDAL** | **LA9 4LY**

Farrer's is a traditional tea and coffee house with an old-fashioned sleek black exterior, bay windows and gold signage. Inside, it has the feel of an old apothecary with enormous tins of a vast array of tea and coffee varieties, sold by helpful and informative staff.

Enjoy many of Farrer's special varieties of tea and coffee in their café area with its glowing woodburner and old portraiture on the walls. Soups, sandwiches, pastries and traditional dishes are served in this simple, specialist store. If you don't want to stop, takeaway drinks are also available.

ADDRESS

13 Stricklandgate
LA9 4LY

PHONE

015397 31707

NEAR HERE

Plumgarths Farm Shop (p153)

The Moon (p73)

The Bakery at No.4 (p70)

Rattle Gill Café

PLACES TO EAT | AMBLESIDE | LA22 9DU

The Rattle Gill Café provides hearty, home cooked goodness in the beautiful surroundings of Ambleside. Baking fresh cakes each day, they also offer their famous Cake Platter; 5 different slices of cake for sweet enthusiasts. The menu offers extensive vegetarian options from homemade soups and veggie chilli to baked potatoes and toated sandwiches. They also have a special each day.

The Rattle Gill's teas and coffees are all fair-trade and often organic. Vibrant fruit smoothies, milkshakes and juices are also available. The café is rustic in style with a large bay window and seating outside on warmer days.

ADDRESS

2 Bridge Street
LA22 9DU

PHONE

015394 31321

NEAR HERE

Push Cartel (p116)

Wateredge Inn (p48)

Beer (p147)

Grange Café

PLACES TO EAT | BORROWDALE | CA12 5XA

Grange Café is wonderfully located in the village of Grange, near the River Derwent where the 1675 double-arched bridge still impresses visitors. The café offers light lunches and sweet treats and has seating both inside and out where you can marvel at the mountains rising high above you on both sides.

The surrounding area is filled with fantastic walks and this makes Grange Café the perfect spot for refreshment. On a cold day you can enjoy local spiced sticky toffee pudding with custard and in the summer nothing beats quality cream tea.

ADDRESS

Grange View
CA12 5XA

PHONE

017687 77077

NEAR HERE

Honister Slate Mine (p113)

Derwentwater (p25)

Buttermere (p23)

Sarah's

PLACES TO EAT | COCKERMOUTH | CA13 9LU

Sarah's in Cockermouth is a simply furnished, contemporary craft café offering high quality teas and coffees alongside a selection of home-baked scones, cakes and light lunches. Service is warm and friendly and the atmosphere is relaxed.

Sarah's is popular with walkers in the area who like a casual environment for a hot drink or a bowl of soup after a hike. The café also sells a collection of local crafts from ceramics to candles and a range of Sarah's own condiments from relishes to chutneys.

ADDRESS

62 Main Street
CA13 9LU

PHONE

01900 824000

NEAR HERE

The New Bookshop (p118)

The Bitter End (p56)

The Shining Tree (p121)

Syke Farm Tearoom

PLACES TO EAT | BUTTERMERE | CA13 9XA

Syke Farm Tea Room is a rustic, farmhouse style café. The farm specialises in Ayrshire dairy cows which means that some of the freshest, regionally renowned ice cream is made and served here. This is the perfect indulgence after a walk around the hypnotically beautiful Buttermere Lake.

Syke Farm Tea Room serves quality food in a casual, family style environment. Home-baked cakes and scones are delicious and opulent and the food is homemade, with light dishes such as soup of the day and sandwiches on the menu. Outside you can breathe in the beauty of the surrounding countryside and enjoy the staggering views.

ADDRESS

Syke Farm
CA13 9XA

PHONE

017687 70277

NEAR HERE

Grange Café (p97)

Crummock Water (p24)

Lingholm Kitchen (p62)

Lucia's

PLACES TO EAT | AMBLESIDE | LA22 9SY

Lucia's is a takeaway coffee shop and bakery in the heart of the Lake District. Home-cooking is the key here and everything from brownies and croissants to sandwiches can be taken away for your picnic or hike in the stunning surrounding countryside.

This unassuming little takeaway café serves a great range of hot drinks from delicious locally roasted coffees to luxurious hot chocolates. The menu changes regularly but offers items like banana bread, Cumberland sausage rolls, cheese scones, spinach and goats cheese tarts and rich tray-bakes.

ADDRESS

College Street
LA22 9SY

PHONE

07874 056187

NEAR HERE

The Jumble Room (p74)

Baldry's (p87)

The Herdy Shop (p130)

Jasper's

PLACES TO EAT | KESWICK | CA12 5HF

Jasper's in Keswick is a vibrant and modern café serving a light menu for breakfast and lunch. With an emphasis on its dog-friendly approach, the sandwich menu is even named after famous furry friends, from the Lassie and Hooch to the Lady and Tramp.

The interior style of Jasper's highlights its love of dogs, with canine artwork and accessories scattered around the walls and even featuring on cushions. Mini leather chesterfield style sofas and wooden tables and chairs furnish the café. The food is homemade and the atmosphere is relaxed and friendly.

ADDRESS

20 Station Street
CA12 5HF

PHONE

017687 73366

NEAR HERE

The Factory Tap (p40)

The Moon (p73)

Comida Food (p72)

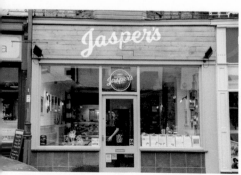

Poppi Red

PLACES TO EAT | **HAWKSHEAD** | **LA22 0NT**

Poppi Red in Hawkshead is a warm and welcoming café and gift shop selling a delicious range of cakes and pastries, freshly ground coffee and big pots of tea. This is the dream of the owner Kim, who spent many years travelling, only to come back and miss the beautiful shops that she had visited on her journeys. She decided to create her own here in Hawkshead.

Uplifting quotes feature on the walls and floral prints, polka dots and stripes in candy colour tones create a breezy, feminine aesthetic. Poppi Red is licensed and sells the locally brewed Hawkshead lager and a local damson gin in the summer months.

ADDRESS
Main Street
LA22 0NT

PHONE
015394 36434

NEAR HERE
Relish Deli (p146)
Waterhead Hotel (p49)
Coniston (p10)

The Crossing Point Café

PLACES TO EAT | KIRKBY LONSDALE | LA6 2AN

Owned and managed by John and Renata Strange, The Crossing Point Café is "the culmination of a dream – an eatery that is all about local produce, the freshest food". Wholesome, home-cooked food is created by the team from carefully selected seasonal ingredients, to ensure exceptional flavour and provenance.

The interior is simple with its woodburner and rustic wooden tables. The wine list has been carefully curated by John and showcases his passion. The Crossing Point creates lovingly prepared, nutritious food in a friendly and relaxed environment. The menu fuses both traditional and contemporary dishes.

ADDRESS

7 Market Square
LA6 2AN

PHONE

015242 98050

NEAR HERE

Ruskin's View (p12)
Kirkby Lonsdale Brewery (p42)
The Sun Inn (p52)

Langwathby Station Café

PLACES TO EAT | LANGWATHBY | CA10 1NB

Langwathby is an attractive and remote train station on the famous Settle to Carlisle line and set within the old waiting room is this intimate little café. Popular with cyclists and walkers who come for their famous cherry scone with cream and jam and home made quiche. Service is friendly and prices are reasonable.

Take shelter from those wet and windy days and warm up in front of their open fire. You might even be lucky enough to see the Flying Scotsman steam engine pass through on its way north. Dogs are welcome.

ADDRESS

Langwathby
CA10 1NB

PHONE

01768 881151

NEAR HERE

Brougham Castle (p33)

The Yard Kitchen (p107)

St. Lawrence's Church (p171)

The Yard Kitchen

PLACES TO EAT | PENRITH | CA11 7LU

The Yard Kitchen is a bright and open, cute little café, which is located at Penrith's Brunswick Yard. White brick walls line the interior where pressed flowers are displayed in frames. There is also a stove, which runs through the cooler months, warming customers alongside hot drinks, such as artisan coffee, hot chocolate and tea.

The Yard Kitchen serve a wide range of soulful dishes, many with a foreign influence. They have good options for vegetarians too and a great choice of cakes and tray bakes. It's a little tricky to find the café, but persevere, as you are likely to enjoy yourselves.

ADDRESS

Brunswick Road
CA11 7LU

PHONE

01768 892002

NEAR HERE

Langwathby Station Café (p106)

The Windmill Cafe (p82)

Buttercup (p119)

No. 6 Finkle Street

PLACES TO EAT | SEDBERGH | LA10 5BZ

No. 6 Finkle Street in Sedburgh has everything you need in terms of home décor. Lighting, kitchen and dining accessories, linens, bedding and a huge range of gifts make this a great browsing and shopping experience. They also operate the Mad Hatters Tea Room where cakes and light lunches can be enjoyed.

You can buy all of their lifestyle stock on their website online. However, to get a real feel for the products, a visit to their shop is best. After stocking up on decorative items for your home, you can treat yourself to afternoon tea at Mad Hatters.

ADDRESS

6 Finkle Street
LA10 5BZ

PHONE

015396 20298

NEAR HERE

Three Hares (p94)

The Dalesman Inn (p41)

Weaving Studio (p127)

The Square Orange Café

PLACES TO EAT | KESWICK | CA12 5AS

The Square Orange offers true continental café culture with a speciality coffee menu. The bar serves a selection of local and continental beers and wines and their specialities are their fresh coffee and authentic Stonebaked Pizza.

The Square Orange has an ethical approach to business with their tea, coffee and sugar being ethically sourced and fair-trade hot chocolate and wine available on request. Live music sets are played every week and are popular with locals and visitors. The interior is reminiscent of a Milanese café, with its large, mirrored wood bar and soft lighting.

ADDRESS

20 St.John's Street

CA12 5AS

PHONE

017687 73888

NEAR HERE

Derwent Pencil Museum (p168)

Kong Adventure (p37)

Theatre by the Lake (p164)

NATURAL BATH
SALTS

NATURAL BATH
SALTS

NATURAL BATH
SALTS

NATURAL BATH
SALTS

CHAPTER FIVE

SHOPPING

Brunswick Yard

SHOPPING | PENRITH | CA11 7JU

The Brunswick Yard is a salvage yard and oriental carpet specialist where all sorts of goods can be found. They sell a selection of antique furniture, architectural salvage items, garden furniture, lights, decorative items and books.

With such a wide range of things for sale, everyone can enjoy a rummage through the shelves and warehouse searching for treasure. After a hunt for goods, you can head to The Yard Kitchen for a spot of lunch or sweet treat. Their cakes and scones are particularly well reputed.

ADDRESS

24 Brunswick Road
CA11 7JU

PHONE

07887 867741

NEAR HERE

Brougham Castle (p33)

Langwathby Station Café (p106)

St Lawrence's Church (p171)

Agnes & Cat

SHOPPING | WINDERMERE | LA23 1BL

Agnes & Cat is a stylish and well-branded cosmetic company, specialising in unique fragrances for natural beauty products. They have two stores; one in Hawkshead and the other in Windermere, both of which showcase their fragrant goods. They sell soy wax scented candles, bath salts, soaps, lip butter, wild hair shampoo and lots of other lovely things.

After a walk through the mountains a long hot bath is hard to beat, so stock up on goods and then completely unwind. The Agnes & Cat shops are attractive and easy to browse through and their products also make great gifts.

ADDRESS
39 Crescent Road
LA23 1BL

PHONE
Not available

NEAR HERE
The Pig (p91)
The Crafty Baa (p45)
Hawkshead Brewery (p32)

Honister Slate Mine

SHOPPING | KESWICK | CA12 5XN

Honister Pass runs between Buttermere and the Borrowdale valley with fantastic views. At the summit is the famous Honister Slate Mine, which has been running for over 300 years. At Honister there are many unique activities to get your blood racing. These include Via Ferrata (extreme cable climbing), mine tours and the infinity bridge.

Also at Honister are a wide range of unusual stylish slate products for sale and a café with simple hot refreshments, ideal after a few hours on or in the mountain. It is known as the wettest place in England, so choose a clear day.

ADDRESS

Honister Pass
CA12 5XN

PHONE

017687 77230

NEAR HERE

Grange Café (p97)

Buttermere (p23)

Lingholm Kitchen (p62)

Galerie D'Art

SHOPPING | BOWNESS ON WINDMERE | LA23 3BY

La Galerie D'Art originally began in Bowness on Windmere and has since branched out to three separate galleries. This gallery shop in Ambleside sells a wide range of prints and original artwork including scenes from the Lake District and romantic pieces of cafés and lovers in France.

As well as art they also sell home accessories such as scented candles, clocks, jewellery, sculptures and gifts. La Galerie D'Art is well laid out and spacious allowing easy browsing during a visit. It's also a great choice for a unique gift or decorative piece for the walls at home.

ADDRESS

Queens Square
LA23 3BY

PHONE

015394 44595

NEAR HERE

Bowness-on-Windermere (p34)

Waterhead Coffee (p64)

Agnes & Cat (p112)

WRS Architectural Antiques

SHOPPING | LOW NEWTON | LA11 6JP

Clive Wilson has been reclaiming antique goods for over 30 years and his massive selection of architectural salvage and antiques is renowned as one of the most diverse and interesting reclamation yards in the UK. All sorts of unique and odd items are on display and for sale here, from cast iron baths to a traditional red post box.

WRS Architectural & Gardening Antiques can be found at Yew Tree Barn alongside artisan studios, gallery space and Harry's café bar. Outside they have a wide selection of decorative items as well as garden furniture and pots.

ADDRESS

Near Grange-over-Sands

LA11 6JP

PHONE

01539 531498

NEAR HERE

Lakeland Motor Museum (p157)

Old Hall Farm (p13)

Haverwaithe Station (p11)

Push Cartel

SHOPPING | AMBLESIDE | LA22 9DT

Push Cartel claims to be "The Lake District's Luxury Cycle Dealership." Their shop looks similar to a gallery space and is pleasant to browse through, with its white walls and bikes hanging like paintings. On display are some of the world's finest bikes and accessories.

The workers are filled with cycle knowledge, gained from professional racing experience and local exploration. They offer a range of services, including bespoke builds, bike fitting, bike workshops and performance analysis. They also serve decent local coffee, which can be enjoyed while looking out over the river Rothay and planning your next hill climb.

ADDRESS
North Road
LA22 9DT

PHONE
015394 31408

NEAR HERE
Rattle Gill Café (p96)
Copper Pot (p80)
LilyLou's (p125)

1786 Leather Goods

SHOPPING | LOW NEWTON | LA11 6JP

1786 Leather Goods is housed alongside multiple creative artisans in the wonderful Yew Tree Barn. Chris McGrath began collecting leather after salvaging hides from a shipwreck dating 1786. His shop shows his collected items and primarily sells vintage luggage of all types; handbags, travelling cases, suitcases and Gladstone bags can all be found.

As well as vintage luggage, there is also a display of uniforms and clothing accessories. The shop is certainly interesting to browse through as it glimpses the past uses of leather and is a bit like a museum. The shop is unique and worth seeking out.

ADDRESS

Near Grange-over-Sands
LA11 6JP

PHONE

01539 531498

NEAR HERE

The Hazelmere (p85)

Cartmel Priory (p170)

Hot Wines (p135)

The New Bookshop

SHOPPING | COCKERMOUTH | CA13 9LQ

Located in the attractive market town of Cockermouth is The New Bookshop. The Bookshop has been running for almost 50 years and is far from new, however it does stock all the latest releases alongside a unique collection of handpicked favourites from local authors and some signed editions too.

They hold regular special events where authors talk about their books; past signings and talks have included Tony Robinson, Richard and Judy and Jason Hewitt to name a few. Also inside the shop is a coffee shop serving light lunches and coffee. It's the ideal spot to relax and get stuck into a new book or meet with a few friends.

ADDRESS

42-44 Main Street
CA13 9LQ

PHONE

01900 822062

NEAR HERE

Sarah's (p98)

Merienda (p81)

The Bitter End (p56)

Buttercup

SHOPPING | KIRKBY STEPHEN | CA17 4QS

Buttercup is a vintage china tearoom and home goods store in the market town of Kirkby Stephen in Cumbria. Artisan coffee and traditional English tea is served in bone china cups alongside moist and luxurious cakes and amongst an eclectic range of home decor products.

Kirkby Stephen is surrounded by spectacular scenery being located in an enviable position between the Lake District National Parks and the Yorkshire Dales. Its location makes it especially attractive to walkers and mountain bikers.

ADDRESS

15 Market Street

CA17 4QS

PHONE

017683 72278

NEAR HERE

Brough Castle (p161)

The Fat Lamb (p57)

Fairfield Mill (p162)

George Fisher

SHOPPING | KESWICK | CA12 5DA

George Fisher have been the go-to outdoor shop for those visiting the Lakes and Keswick for the past 60 years and have recently celebrated 25 years of "The Update" the running of their outdoor enthusiasts magazine. The Shop now covers four floors and stocks the very best outdoor equipment and gear, including specialist camping and climbing equipment, a ski service workshop, Abraham's Café and plenty more.

If you're heading out around the Lakes and need some information, a unique item or some sound advice, then this is the place for you. Expect all the top brands as well as local maps and guides to the area.

ADDRESS

2 Borrowdale Road
CA12 5DA

PHONE

017687 72178

NEAR HERE

Fellpack (p67)

Derwent Pencil Museum (p168)

Theatre by the Lake (p164)

The Shining Tree

SHOPPING | COCKERMOUTH | CA13 9NH

The Shining Tree in Cockermouth is an imaginative independent shop for lovers of the arts, gardens and antiques, founded by Debbie Taylor, a writer and professional gardener with an interest in design and decorative arts.

The stock of The Shining Tree changes frequently and includes art by local painters and photographers, decorative items, statues, trinkets and antiques. The Market Place is often missed when visiting Cockermouth, yet there are plenty of decent eateries and shops that are great for browsing through in the area.

ADDRESS

3 Market Place

CA13 9NH

PHONE

01900 827555

NEAR HERE

The Moon & Sixpence (p79)

The New Bookshop (p118)

Sarah's (p98)

The Red Gecko

SHOPPING | GRASMERE | LA22 9SN

The Red Gecko imports unique hand crafted, artisan products from Bali and the Orient. The owners travel extensively to source products directly from the people who make them and ensure their purchases are made from ethical and responsible sources. The shop is located in the charming village of Grasmere, one of Cumbria's most popular tourist spots.

Their name comes from a rare New Zealand reptile called the Takitimu Gecko, unique to the alpine regions of the Takitimu Mountains in New Zealand's South Island. They have three stores, two in this part of the country and one on the south coast in Brighton.

ADDRESS

Stock Lane
LA22 9SN

PHONE

015394 35112

NEAR HERE

Grasmere Gingerbread Shop (p138)

Lucia's (p100)

Heaton Cooper Studio (p167)

LilyLou's

SHOPPING | AMBLESIDE | LA22 9DG

LilyLou's of Ambleside has over 30 years of floral expertise in shop and here qualified florist Joanne Dann creates beautiful bouquets and displays for weddings and special events. Joanne offers a very personal service and often visits clients and venues to discuss their event and particular arrangements.

The shop in Ambleside showcases examples of bouquets and colour schemes and includes 'The Wedding Room', which contains wedding props for hire. You can customise your bouquet and choose individual decorative pieces to display in your home. This is a beautiful shop to visit and a great choice for special events.

ADDRESS

St. Mary's Lane
LA22 9DG

PHONE

015394 33121

NEAR HERE

Copper Pot (p80)

Push Cartel (p116)

Wateredge Inn (p48)

Half Moon Interiors

SHOPPING | WIGTON | CA7 9NJ

Half Moon Interiors in Wigton stock a wide range of home accessories, furniture, lighting, bedding, baby clothes and nursery furniture. They stock brand names such as Voyage furniture, nursery items from Kidsmill and wooden playthings from Plan Toys to name a few.

The shop has loads of decorative items too, displayed throughout three separate rooms. This is a fine shop for interior designers or for those simply looking for something to spruce up their home with a unique object, such as a giant clock or drawing.

ADDRESS

37 High Street
CA7 9NJ

PHONE

016973 49211

NEAR HERE

Carlisle Cathedral (p165)

The Windmill Café (p82)

The Lakes Distillery (p31)

Squirrel

SHOPPING | ULVERSTON | LA12 7LS

Squirrel is a large homeware and crafts shop located in the pretty market town of Ulverston. The shop has all sorts of unique home furnishings, attractive gifts and materials for creatives. At the back of the shop is a craft area, where visitors can partake in ceramic painting, card making, collaging and other hands on activities.

Squirrel has a great range of products from succulents to lampshades and is worth browsing through when in town. Lots of their stock is created locally and their children's section has kids dining ware, puzzles, games, cuddly toys and puppets.

ADDRESS

43 Market Street
LA12 7LS

PHONE

01229 588028

NEAR HERE

Ford Park (p35)

Bici Café (p71)

Gillam's Tea Room (p65)

The Herdy Shop

SHOPPING | GRASMERE | LA22 9SZ

Herdy is one of the Lake District's best loved brands and is easily recognisable from its smiling sheep's face branding and bold colour schemes. The brand was inspired by the area's Herdwick sheep and was first seen on mugs, pin badges and keyrings.

Herdy now export to over 400 retailers worldwide and have three shops in the north of England. Their range of products now includes tableware, bags and accessories, gifts, jewellery, baby clothes and much more. This shop in attractive Grasmere sells all the Herdy products you could ever desire, ewe wont be disappointed.

ADDRESS

College Street
LA22 9SZ

PHONE

01539 435051

NEAR HERE

The Jumble Room (p74)

Emmas Dell (p75)

Rydal Water (p29)

Parma Violet

SHOPPING | KIRKBY LONSDALE | LA6 2AH

Parma Violet sits on Main Street in the quaint Victorian market town of Kirkby Lonsdale in Cumbria. The shop offers an eclectic mix of gifts, toys and vintage goods. The shop was named after its previous incarnation as the village sweet shop and has been doing a fine trade since 2005.

Kirkby Lonsdale is a picturesque and historic market town on the River Lune. The enchanting network of mellow stone edifices and narrow cobbled lanes, framed by a pastoral landscape make this a popular destination with photographers. If you are visiting, be sure to see the Devil's Bridge which dates back to 1370.

ADDRESS

45 Main Street
LA6 2AH

PHONE

015242 72585

NEAR HERE

Ruskin's View (p12)

The Plough (p44)

The Sun Inn (p52)

CHAPTER SIX

FOOD
SHOPS

Cartmel Cheeses and Bakery

FOOD SHOPS | **CARTMEL** | **LA11 6PN**

Cartmel Cheeses & Bakery is one of the delightful businesses nestled within Unsworth's Yard. Unsurprisingly given its name, the shop specialises in a wide range of British, Irish and French cheeses and freshly baked goods. It makes an ideal stop to gather a few picnic nibbles for a day out exploring the Lake District.

The village of Cartmel has become a a popular culinary destination, best known for its Michelin starred L'Enclume restaurant and this shop holds its own amongst such prestigious company. Be sure to pop in to Unsworth's Yard Brewery next door for a tasting before you head out into the countryside.

ADDRESS

Grange Over Sands
LA11 6PN

PHONE

015395 34307

NEAR HERE

Hot Wines (p135)

Cartmel Priory (p170)

The Hazelmere (p85)

Low Sizergh Barn

FOOD SHOPS | **KENDAL** | **LA8 8AE**

Records show a farm has existed on the site of Low Sizergh Barn since the 13th century. Once the home farm of Sizergh Castle, the farm today is one of the largest providers of dairy produce in the region. The welfare of the animals and the natural environment is of paramount importance to the farm.

Alongside a beautiful 17th century barn farm shop offering quality produce with provenance, the café above the milking sheds offers cooked breakfasts, light lunches and farmhouse teas. Every afternoon around 3.30pm the farm's cows come in to be milked and the café's large windows provide the perfect viewing gallery.

ADDRESS

Low Sizergh Barn

LA8 8AE

PHONE

01539 560426

NEAR HERE

The Strickland Arms (p43)

Hare and Hounds (p51)

Kitridding Farm Shop (p154)

Hotwines

FOOD SHOPS | CARTMEL | LA11 6PN

Hotwines specialises in the finest wines, spirits and liqueurs from around the world with a unique "try before you buy" available across much of the range. Expert knowledge and attention to high quality customer service is their focus, as is small artisan producers, regional liquors and single estate wines.

Situated in the heart of the medieval village of Cartmel and overlooked by the beautiful 12th century Priory, Unsworth's Yard has been owned by the same family since 1922 and is now home to several of the village's many fine food producers and sellers, including Hotwines.

ADDRESS

Grange Over Sands
LA11 6PN

PHONE

015395 36025

NEAR HERE

The Hazelmere (p85)

Rogan & Company (p66)

Cartmel Priory (p170)

Grasmere Gingerbread Shop

FOOD SHOPS | GRASMERE | LA22 9SW

The Grasmere Gingerbread Shop was established by Victorian cook Sarah Nelson in 1854. The reputation of her delicious gingerbread quickly gained traction and today the shop's famous clientele includes Hollywood actor Tom Cruise. This tiny shop was Sarah Nelson's Church Cottage home and remains almost untouched to this day.

Sarah Nelson's original gingerbread recipe is hand-written on parchment and safely stored away in a secure bank safe in the Lake District. The only person alive today who knows the recipe is Andrew Hunter, a partner in the business, who mixes and bakes the gingerbread fresh every day.

ADDRESS
Church Cottage
LA22 9SW

PHONE
015394 35428

NEAR HERE
Lucia's (p100)

The Red Gecko (p124)

The Herdy Shop (p130)

1657 Chocolate House

FOOD SHOPS | KENDAL | LA9 4TX

1657 Chocolate House in Kendal, Cumbria is believed to have been built in the 1630's, originally as a private home. Today it is a chocolate retailer selling 100 different kinds of loose chocolates. They offer a customisation service, where you can pick your chocolates and boxes to create the perfect gift or personal indulgence.

1657 Chocolate House is a beautiful building with a traditional interior. Inside a tearoom serves a multitude of hot chocolate varieties (16 at last count), and a range of sweet and savoury food. The shop is a treasure trove for chocolate lovers.

ADDRESS

54 Branthwaite Brow

LA9 4TX

PHONE

01539 740702

NEAR HERE

Comida Food (p72)

The Moon (p73)

Plumgarths Farm Shop (p153)

Dales Traditional Butchers

FOOD SHOPS | KIRKBY LONSDALE | LA6 2AU

Dales Traditional Butchers have been supplying quality, locally reared meats for over 100 years in Kirkby Lonsdale. Established in 1906 by Herbert Dale, the produce comes from local farms who supply only the highest quality meats from Cumbrian and Lancastrian land.

The produce ranges from traditional meats, pies and puddings to fine cheeses and fresh vegetables at Dales Traditional Butchers. Staff are friendly and experienced and their award winning pies are all produced in house to traditional recipes, using only the best locally sourced ingredients.

ADDRESS

2 Market Street
LA6 2AU

PHONE

015242 71278

NEAR HERE

Ruskin's View (p12)

Kitridding Farm Shop (p154)

Kirkby Lonsdale Brewery (p42)

Fat Flour

FOOD SHOPS | GRANGE-OVER-SANDS | LA11 7NY

Fat Flour is a family-run artisan bakery in Cartmel. While traditional artisan techniques are an integral part of Fat Flour, they do use advanced technology alongside their hand-crafted methods. Baguettes, ficelles, dinner rolls, sandwich breads, breadsticks, boules, pullman loaves, focaccia and freeform breads are often available from around 20 varieties of breads made each day.

The patisseries created at Fat Flour are popular choices and the sourdough pizza bread is becoming a local favourite. John Dixon is the young baker behind the brand and his enthusiasm for quality bread is palpable.

ADDRESS

127 Station Road
LA11 7NY

PHONE

015395 59069

NEAR HERE

Rogan & Company (p66)

The Hazelmere (p85)

Cartmel Cheeses (p133)

Baba Ganoush

FOOD SHOPS | KENDAL | LA9 4AB

Baba Ganoush is an award-winning foodshop, canteen and bakehouse situated in the Cumbrian market town of Kendal. The Bakehouse is the central creative hub of Baba Ganoush. All of the baking and a great deal of the fresh food is prepared here. The simple, unfussy and contemporary interior has a woodburner and relaxed ambience.

Big salads, melts, wraps and home-cooked comfort food are served alongside innovative vegetarian options and salad boxes at Baba Ganoush. Their decadent cake counter displays sumptuous and irresistible offerings.

ADDRESS

Unit 4, Berrys Yard, 27 Finkle Street

LA9 4AB

PHONE

01539 738210

NEAR HERE

The Bakery at No.4 (p70)

The Moon (p73)

1657 Chocolate House (p139)

Staff of Life

FOOD SHOPS | KENDAL | LA9 4AB

Staff of Life is a family-run artisan bakery in Kendal. Hand-made bread is offered fresh every day and customers enjoy purchasing the bread often straight from the oven. Breads are mixed the night before and left to slowly rise using little yeast or salt. They also pride themselves on their sourdoughs which use local damson and elderflower ingredients.

Wholemeals, light ryes with caraway, 100% rye, sourdoughs, filled Italian style breads, Rustica, Stromboli, as well as seasonal specials, scones and a large range of cakes are created and sold at Staff of Life. Baking courses are also run from the bakery.

ADDRESS

2 Berry's Yard
LA9 4AB

PHONE

01539 738606

NEAR HERE

Baba Ganoush (p144)

Farrer's of Kendal (p95)

The Moon (p73)

Relish

FOOD SHOPS | **HAWKSHEAD** | **LA22 0NZ**

The Hawkshead Relish Company is an artisan producer of award-winning preserves. The range of over 120 relishes, pickles and preserves are handmade in small batches, using traditional open pans and locally sourced ingredients.

A traditional, 16th century Lakeland building in the heart of Hawkshead houses Relish's full collection of handmade creations, and was the original premises of Relish. From their award-winning Nettle Jelly to their popular Westmorland Chutney (made to a traditional Cumbrian recipe), Relish is receiving numerous accolades for their delicious produce.

ADDRESS
The Square
LA22 0NZ

PHONE
015394 36614

NEAR HERE
Factory Tap (p40)
Farrer's of Kendal (p95)
The Punch Bowl (p53)

Beer

FOOD SHOPS | **AMBLESIDE** | **LA22 0BZ**

Beer in Ambleside was founded by award-winning self taught brewer Kelly Barbenson, offering a large range of regional and national craft beers. The shop also offers an innovative 'filling station'. This is a counter pressure filling machine that allows beers, that may not already be bottled, to be containerised on the premises and taken away by customers.

The staff at Beer in Ambleside are knowledgeable, friendly and enthusiastic about their extensive selection of quality beers and samples are often available to taste under their guidance. This is an establishment where the passion of the founders is palpable.

ADDRESS

8 Kelsick Road
LA22 0BZ

PHONE

015394 22290

NEAR HERE

Copper Pot (p80)

Waterhead Coffee (p64)

Rydal Water (p29)

Notes

Tried our app?

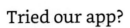

Tony Harrison

FOOD SHOPS | COCKERMOUTH | CA13 9LU

Tony Harrison is a butchers in Cockermouth and provides native breed, free range, pasture fed, dry aged meat carefully selected from small farmers who care. Their meat is seasonal and they source directly from the farms, ensuring that the meat is fully traceable and of a high quality.

Tony Harrison's shop has a friendly, knowledgable and accommodating approach, making it a popular choice with locals. Their pies are locally renowned and they also offer homemade ready-meals for people to take-away. BBQ food such as their kebabs and burgers make for easy summer catering, for those with more carnivorous palates.

ADDRESS

82 Main Street
CA13 9LU

PHONE

01900 823164

NEAR HERE

Merienda (p81)

The Lakes Distillery (p31)

The Pheasant (p39)

Low Howgill Butchers & Deli

FOOD SHOPS | KESWICK | CA12 5DQ

Low Howgil Butchers & Deli is an award-winning destination food shop serving high quality meats, pies and delicatessen produce. With an on-site bakery, the shop offers some of the freshest pies around, always incorporating their own meat into the recipes. Their traditional meats and associated produce often have a seasonal twist.

The meat here at Low Howgil Butchers and Deli comes from the family farm and ingredients are from local farms wherever possible. The farm to fork ethos has made the shop a popular choice in the region. The interior is contemporary and the branding is stylish.

ADDRESS

34 Lake Road
CA12 5DQ

PHONE

017687 72666

NEAR HERE

Morrels (p90)

Jasper's (p101)

Kong Adventure (p37)

The Little Ice Cream Shop

FOOD SHOPS | **HAWKSHEAD** | **LA22 0NZ**

The Little Ice Cream Shop is Hawkshead's first specialist artisan ice cream shop. Serving 22 delicious and unique flavours of pure indulgence, their ice cream is made by a local farm who have been making luxurious ice cream from their small dairy herd since 1948.

Alongside their popular ice cream flavours which range from salted caramel and bonfire night toffee to lemon meringue, juicy sorbets are also served for a more refreshing alternative. A selection of locally roasted coffee, teas and home-baked cakes and tray bakes are all available to eat-in or take-away.

ADDRESS
Laburnum House
LA22 0NZ

PHONE
01593 512345

NEAR HERE
Poppi Red (p104)
Waterhead Hotel (p49)
Bowness-on-Windermere (p34)

Plumgarths Farm Shop

FOOD SHOPS | KENDAL | LA8 8LX

Plumgarths Farm Shop offers a one-stop shop for the best local farm produce. From meat, dressings, preserves, ice-creams, ales, breads, baked goods, fruit and vegetables, all items stocked are from local and passionate small-scale producers.

Next door to Plumgarths Farm Shop is the popular Two Sisters Café, serving hearty breakfasts, light lunches and opulent afternoon teas. The sister team are passionate about baking and creating a welcoming environment to enjoy their home-cooked food. The café is simple in style with lots of light and a woodburner for colder days.

ADDRESS

Crook Road
LA8 8LX

PHONE

01539 736300

NEAR HERE

Farrer's of Kendal (p95)

The Bakery at No.4 (p70)

Staff of Life (p145)

Kitridding Farm Shop

FOOD SHOPS | KIRKBY LONSDALE | LA6 2QA

Kitridding Farm Shop is an award-winning family business selling farm-to-table, native breed, traditionally butchered meats from their farm shop in Kirkby Lonsdale. All their animals are traditionally home reared without intensive, industrial farming methods. Their animals graze in fields between Spring and late Autumn and are housed during the winter months and fed on grass harvested in the summer.

The provenance of their produce is something Kitridding Farm Shop feel passionately about. Humane practices are part of their ethos and ensured at every stage of production including within their family-run abattoir.

ADDRESS

Kitridding
LA6 2QA

PHONE

01539 567484

NEAR HERE

The Plough (p44)

Dales Traditional Butchers (p140)

Kirkby Lonsdale (p20)

CHAPTER SEVEN

CULTURE

The Rum Story

CULTURE | WHITEHAVEN | CA28 7DN

The Rum Story is a museum in Whitehaven set in the original 1785 rum shop and which takes you on an interactive journey through the history of the spirit. They have wonderful themed rooms filled with surprises throughout; the rooms include a rainforest, an African village, a slave ship, and a Coopers workshop.

You can have a taste of the famed Rum and purchase bottles and rum butter from their gift shop. There is also a coffee shop in the bright and airy courtyard, which is covered from the elements. The Rum Story is a hidden gem, worth discovering.

ADDRESS

27 Lowther Street
CA28 7DN

PHONE

01946 592933

NEAR HERE

St Bees (p21)

Muncaster Castle (p172)

Ravenglass Station (p30)

Lakeland Motor Museum

CULTURE | ULVERSTON | LA12 8TA

Lakeland Motor Museum has over 30,000 exhibits from around the world and chronicles the history of motoring through the twentieth century. The museum is a marvellous homage to the internal combustion engine and is housed in a converted mill. On display are cars, motorbikes, pedal cars, bicycles and the occasional unique machine.

The museum also sports numerous motor-related artefacts such as vintage petrol pumps and special collections relating to the Campbell Bluebird and Isle of Man TT display. Many hours can be spent marvelling at the beauty and design of bygone ages, with classics from Europe and the US.

ADDRESS

Old Blue Mill, Backbarrow
LA12 8TA

PHONE

015395 30400

NEAR HERE

Old Hall Farm (p13)

Stott Park Bobbin Mill (p14)

Haverwaithe Station (p11)

The Old Grammar School

CULTURE | HAWKSHEAD | LA22 0NT

The Old Grammar School in Hawkshead is a marvelous historical site in the heart of the Lake District. It was originally founded in 1585 by the Archbishop of York as a school and taught Latin grammar, ancient history and the sciences. It was a unique Tudor school, governed by a charter from Queen Elizabeth I.

The present museum is almost untouched and exhibits the richest display of school life back in the 16th Century, making it a must see for history fans. Paintings of great masters, inkpots and vandalized pews all stand strong within the pretty two-storey house. The Old Grammar School is an interesting visit for all.

ADDRESS
Main Street
LA22 0NT

PHONE
015394 36735

NEAR HERE
Relish Deli (p146)
Poppi Red (p104)
Waterhead Hotel (p49)

The Dent Heritage Centre

CULTURE | DENT | LA10 5QJ

Beautifully designed by local labourers, the Dent Heritage Centre provides a wealth of information about the working lives and history of the Dales area. The artefacts and objects have been carefully collected and lovingly restored, providing a fascinating glimpse into days gone by.

Discover how the rural communities have made a living from the land over the centuries and how they survived through some harsh times in this remote area. The centre offers a wealth of detail on the railways, the folklore, daily life and customs that have shaped the Dales into the rich experience it is today.

ADDRESS

Dent
LA10 5QJ

PHONE

01539 625800

NEAR HERE

Fairfield Mill (p162)

No. 6 Finkle Street (p108)

Weaving Studio (p127)

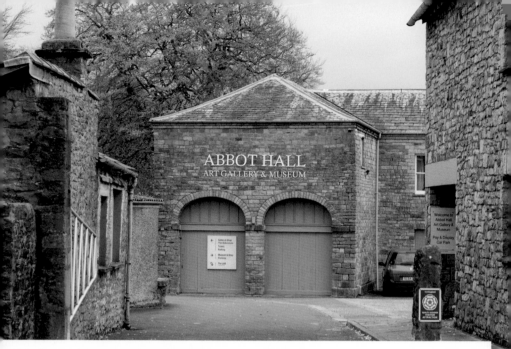

Abbot Hall Art Gallery

CULTURE | KENDAL | LA9 5AL

Abbot Hall Art Gallery is a Grade I listed museum and gallery that was built in 1759 by Colonel George Wilson, whose family owned a large house and country estate nearby. The gallery showcases contemporary and historic art including portraits by 18th-century local artist George Romney as well as 300 years of British landscape paintings.

The building was rescued by locals having fallen into disrepair in the 1950s and recently won the Art Gallery of the Year Cumbria Life Culture Awards. The gallery is located beside the river in the heart of the Cumbrian town of Kendal.

ADDRESS

Kirkland

LA9 5AL

PHONE

01539 722464

NEAR HERE

The Moon (p73)

The Bakery at No.4 (p70)

1657 Chocolate House (p139)

Brough Castle

CULTURE | BROUGH | CA17 4EJ

Standing on a ridge along the Stanmore Pass is the impressive remains of Brough Castle beside the river Swindale Beck. The castle was built on the site of a Roman fort and its towering keep dates from about 1200. It was an easy target for the Scots and was raided frequently.

The Clifford Family extended its living quarters on the site shortly after 1510 and when celebrating Christmas with a great party in 1521 they were accidently burned down. In the 17th century, Lady Ann Clifford restored much of the castle and you can still see much of this restoration today. A walk around Brough Castle is pleasant and interesting.

ADDRESS
Rosemount
CA17 4EJ

PHONE
0370 3331181

NEAR HERE
Brougham Castle (p33)
Buttercup (p119)
The Fat Lamb (p57)

Fairfield Mill

CULTURE | SEDBERGH | LA10 5LW

Fairfield Mill is a Victorian Woollen Mill located in the heart of the Yorkshire Dales. Originally built in 1837, the mill was the last surviving woollen mill in the Western Dales and produced textiles for 156 years. The mill was lovingly restored in 2001 with new life has been breathed in to this charming industrial structure and the rugged stone exterior.

Today, there are four floors of exhibition space showcasing local heritage and textile arts. Step back in time to understand how the mill operated and the products it made. There is also a cafe on site and parking is free.

ADDRESS
Garsdale Road
LA10 5LW

PHONE
015396 21958

NEAR HERE
Three Hares (p94)
The Dalesman Inn (p41)
The Dent Heritage Centre
(p159)

Blackwell, The Arts & Crafts House

CULTURE | BOWNESS | LA23 3JT

Blackwell, The Arts & Crafts House was completed in 1900 and is an outstanding example of British architecture. The large house overlooks Lake Windermere and is full of rare impressive features, including hessian wall hangings, carved wooden paneling and stained glass windows.

The gardens are laid out as a series of terraces and offer fantastic views and the flowerbeds and long sweeping lawn enhance this stunning location. The shop on-site has plenty of gifts for those after something special to take home and regular exhibitions add to the displays and sit well with the impressive furnishings.

ADDRESS
Bowness-on-Windermere
LA23 3JT

PHONE
01539 446139

NEAR HERE
Bowness-on-Windermere (p34)
Lakeland Motor Museum (p157)
Haverwaithe Station (p11)

Theatre by the Lake

CULTURE | KESWICK | CA12 5DJ

Theatre by the Lake is quite possibly the best-located theatre in Britain, a short walk from Derwentwater on the edge of Keswick. It first opened in 1999 and has two stages; the Main House with 400 seats and the Studio with 100 seats. The Theatre present nine of their own productions throughout the year and their Christmas plays are a favourite for the whole family.

The Theatre by the Lake is also home to the Spotlight Café and Bar as well as the Lakeside Café Restaurant which is open from 9-9 daily, and is the perfect spot to view the lake and fells beyond. Performances run almost every day and make a visit to Keswick more memorable.

ADDRESS

Lake Road
CA12 5DJ

PHONE

017687 74411

NEAR HERE

Lingholm Kitchen (p62)

Derwent Pencil Museum (p168)

Kong Adventure (p37)

Carlisle Cathedral

CULTURE | CARLISLE | CA3 8TZ

A visit to Carlisle Cathedral is surely memorable. The ceiling glistens with gold and the ancient medieval choir stalls have withstood time and are worth running your hand along the smooth surfaces. It's gone through a series of building phases and has just been awarded a grant to re-build the dining hall known as the Frantry building.

A church has stood here for around 900 years and there are plenty of features to take you on an historic journey. To gain an even better in-depth knowledge of the nooks and crannies you can take a tour of the Cathedral. Evensong is sung daily in the church and there is also a daily service.

ADDRESS

7 Abbey Street
CA3 8TZ

PHONE

01228 548151

NEAR HERE

Lanercost Priory (p173)

Half Moon Interiors (p126)

The Windmill Café (p82)

Lancaster Castle

CULTURE | LANCASTER | LA1 1YJ

Lancaster Castle is historically fascinating and dates back to Roman times, when its commanding position on the hill overlooking the town of Lancaster and the River Lune protected the area from invasion. The castle today offers insight into the nation's religious and cultural beliefs throughout the centuries.

Lancaster Castle is open daily for guided tours and visitors can enjoy the courtyard spaces, external views of the historic building, two small exhibition spaces and the giftshop without charge. Public access to the interiors of the castle buildings is by guided tour only.

ADDRESS

Castle Park
LA1 1YJ

PHONE

01524 64998

NEAR HERE

The Plough (p44)

Highwayman (p59)

The Fenwick Arms (p60)

Heaton Cooper Studio & Gallery

CULTURE | GRASMERE | LA22 9SX

Established in 1905, the Heaton Cooper Studio is a thriving, family-run art gallery, bookshop, exhibition space and attractive modern café called Mathilde's, which overlooks the village green of Grasmere and out to the hills beyond.

Heaton Cooper Studio is home to the Heaton Cooper family set of artists and it exhibits past and present work from the family tree, including prints and paintings of the beautiful surrounding area. There is also a well-stocked art shop on site with world-class materials, for creatives. If you're visiting Grasmere, then it's well worth a visit.

ADDRESS
Broadgate
LA22 9SX

PHONE
015394 35280

NEAR HERE
The Herdy Shop (p130)
Lucia's (p100)
The Jumble Room (p74)

Derwent Pencil Museum

CULTURE | KESWICK | CA12 5NG

After the discovery of graphite in the Barrowdale Valley the birth of the pencil was imminent. The Cumberland Pencil Company created its first pencil in Keswick in 1832 and the first factory was built the same year. The Derwent Pencil Museum is located beside the old factory and tells the story of the interesting journey the company has been through.

Highlights include a replica graphite mine, secret WW2 pencils with hidden maps, one of the largest pencils in the world and miniature pencil sculptures. On site is a large fine art retail shop, where you can purchase all the creative drawing materials you desire.

ADDRESS

Southey Works
CA12 5NG

PHONE

017687 73626

NEAR HERE

Kong Adventure (p37)

The Square Orange Café (p109)

Morrels (p90)

Cathedral Cavern

CULTURE | AMBLESIDE | LA22 9PB

Cathedral Cavern, an explorer's dream, is a network of old slate quarries, located just above the Little Langdale Valley. The highlight of the quarry is the grand main chamber. It reaches up over 40 foot high and has two large openings that let in generous amounts of natural light so that you can see quite easily the pool of water and central column.

To reach Cathedral Cavern is relatively straightforward, however, be sure to take a torch for the tunnels and wear sturdy boots, as the paths are often slippery and wet. A visit is exciting for all ages and the acoustics are unique in the main cavern, so sing your heart out.

ADDRESS

LA22 9PB

PHONE
Not available

NEAR HERE
Rydal Water (p29)

Chesters (p63)

Wateredge Inn (p48)

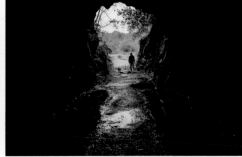

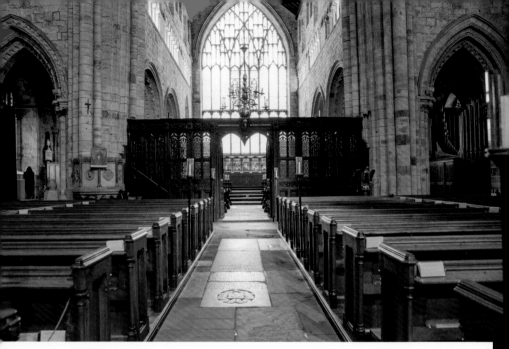

Cartmel Priory

CULTURE | CARTMEL | LA11 6PU

Cartmel Priory is an extremely impressive church for such a small parish and has an impressive history to match. War, raids and ruin have all played a part in the Priory's existence. Yet today its lofty roof, delicate stained glass windows and grand altar radiate calm and peace.

The Priory has a unique square belfry tower, which has been constructed diagonally across the original tower and is the only one of its kind in the UK. Other parts of interest include intricate carvings and engravings, bullet holes and ancient choir stalls. Cartmel is a wonderfully attractive small village and the church is a must when visiting.

ADDRESS
The Vicarage
LA11 6PU

PHONE
015395 36261

NEAR HERE
Rogan & Company (p66)
Hot Wines (p135)
Fat Flour (p141)

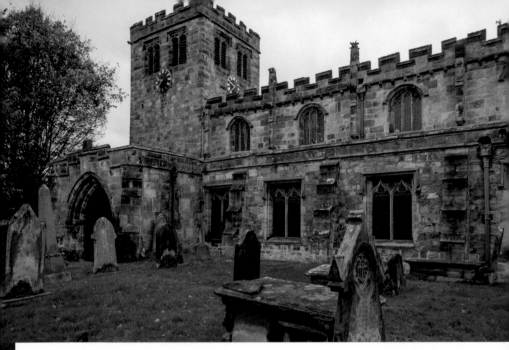

St Lawrence's Church

CULTURE | APPLEBY | CA16 6QN

St Lawrence's Church in Appleby-in-Westmorland is an active Anglican parish church in the deanery of Appleby. The lower part of the tower on St Lawrence's Church dates from about 1150 and the main body originates from the 14th and 15th centuries.

As well as many of her castle estates Lady Anne Clifford restored the church and rebuilt the north chapel. She even designed her own memorial tomb which you can see when visiting. St Lawrence's Church is united with six other local churches that form the benefice of Heart of Eden. It's an impressive building with grand arches and is worth visiting when in Appleby.

ADDRESS
Boroughgate
CA16 6QN

PHONE
017683 61269

NEAR HERE
Brough Castle (p161)
Brougham Castle (p33)
The Fat Lamb (p57)

Muncaster Castle

CULTURE | RAVENGLASS | CA18 1RQ

Muncaster Castle is an historic haunted building, surrounded by tranquil Himalayan gardens and bluebell woods. It overlooks the beautiful Eskdale Valley and the river Esk and is a short drive from Ravenglass town, for which it may have acted as a fort in the past. The Pennington family owns the Castle and they have lived at Muncaster for at least 800 years.

Today the site includes a hawk and owl centre, meadow vole maze and adventure playgrounds, a café, gift shop and accommodation. They run exciting events and festivals throughout the year and the castle is often used for ceremonies and functions.

ADDRESS

Muncaster
CA18 1RQ

PHONE

01229 717614

NEAR HERE

Ravenglas Station (p30)

St Bees (p21)

The Byre Tearooms (p83)

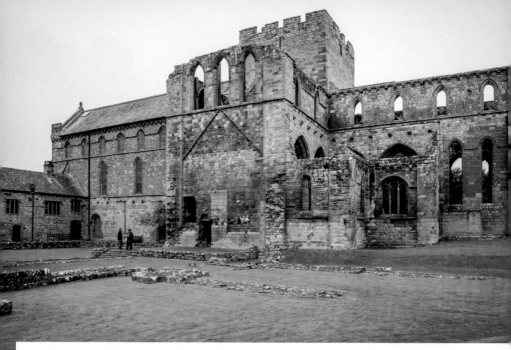

Lanercost Priory

CULTURE | LANERCOST | CA8 2HQ

The best preserved of all Cumbria's priories, Lanercost is a dramatic and impressive edifice. It suffered many attacks over the years from the Scots due to its close proximity to Hadrian's Wall. Considering the frequent attacks, the east end of the noble 13th Century Church survived to its full height and the dramatic triple tiers of arches are still admired by those who visit.

Lanercoast Priory includes a working church, the ruins of the monastic buildings, tombs, Roman stonework and altars. There's a lot to see and do at this English Heritage site and there is a tearoom 100 yards from the Priory, ideal for refreshment.

ADDRESS
Near Brampton
CA8 2HQ

PHONE
01697 73030

NEAR HERE
Lanercost Tearoom (p86)
Carlisle Cathedral (p165)
Langwathby Station Café (p106)

CHAPTER EIGHT

MAP & INDEX

Index

Notes

Tried our app?

bestofengland.com/app

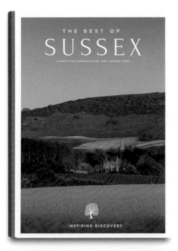

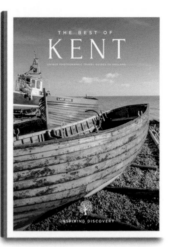

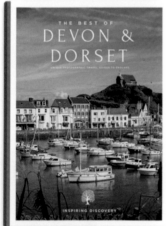

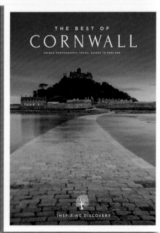

Meet the family

Honest Recommendations & Hidden Gems

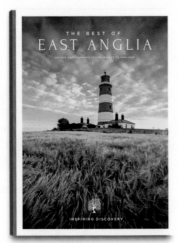

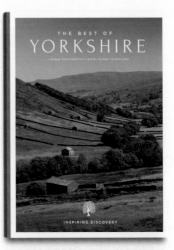

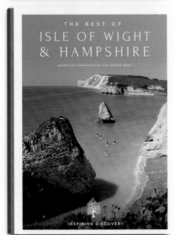

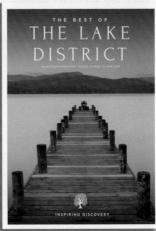

Enjoy 10% off your next purchase using the code: "bestoffriends"

www.bestofengland.com/books

Editor's Picks

A596

Maryport

13

9

Cockermouth

4

19

Whitehaven

Buttermere

Gosforth

A595

Ravenglass

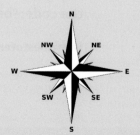